331·114

# FOREWORD

This research paper provides what I, as Chairman of the Skills Task Force, believe to be the most comprehensive analysis ever of our country's skill needs and how well we are meeting them. It contains the evidence base for the Task Force's final report Skills for All: proposals for a National Skills Agenda.

Our ambitious programme of research and information gathering entailed interviews with over 23,000 employers, consultations and case studies relating to key sectors of the economy, projections of future employment, analyses of rates of return on skills, international comparisons with our key competitors, and comprehensive literature surveys. The methodology we have employed offers a basis for the skills assessments that the new National Learning and Skills Council will undertake in future.

The value of this body of evidence goes beyond its use to us in defining the national skills agenda. Findings published here and in our series of research papers will be a resource for those planning our education and training provision, and those advising individuals and employers on training and development. I am pleased that the Government is already using this material in implementing our recommendations to create better informed demand for learning, in drawing up guidance to agencies such as RDAs about skills priorities, and in the industry skills dialogues with National Training Organisations.

But this report must only be the first milestone in our quest to use intelligence to end skills shortages and skills gaps. I have no doubt that the new LSC will build on our work to improve continuously on this template for a national skills assessment and to spread more widely that knowledge and understanding of the link between learning and jobs.

# ACKNOWLEDGEMENTS

The Chairman and the members of the Skills Task Force would like to record their thanks to all those who contributed to the analysis contained in this report and especially those members of the Skills Task Force Research Group listed at Annex B. Thanks go to all the researchers who provided the evidence referred to in the report, in particular those who undertook projects at the specific request of the Task Force.  Special thanks go to Geoff Mason from the National Institute of Economic and Social Research who has given valuable advice in preparing the report. While all these individuals have contributed greatly to the report they do not bear any responsibility for the analysis or views expressed in it.

# Contents

**Foreword** ............................................................................................................ **3**

**Acknowledgements** .......................................................................................... **4**

**Contents** ............................................................................................................ **5**

**Executive Summary** ........................................................................................ **11**


Chapter 1

**Introduction** .................................................................................................... **16**

Sets out the purpose of the report and highlights the ideal way of identifying the priority skill needs of the economy. Acknowledges that we cannot achieve this ideal and outlines the eclectic approach to analysis taken in the report.

- **Our approach**                                                        **17**
- **Analyses based on rates of return**                                   **17**
- **Trends in jobs and earnings**                                         **18**
- **Trends in skills supply**                                             **18**
- **Direct measures of skills and employer-based research**              **19**


Chapter 2

**What we mean by skill and why skills are important** ............................ **21**

Defines what we mean by skill and identifies the main skills types considered in the report. Summarises the evidence on the benefits of skills to the individual, to firms and the economy and society at large.

- **Skills - definitions & conceptual issues**                            **21**
    - Skills hierarchies                                                  **21**
    - Complexity and discretion                                           **22**
    - Cognitive and manual skills                                         **22**
    - Economic worth of skills and their application to jobs             **23**
    - Generic/vocational skills and personal attributes                  **24**

- **Skill formation**                                                     **24**

- **The role of skills**                                                  **25**
    - The benefits of skills to the individual                           **26**
    - The benefits of skills to firms                                     **28**
    - The benefits to the economy                                        **29**

- **Summary**                                                             **31**

Chapter 3
## Changes in the nature of jobs and skill requirements ........................................ **35**

Outlines trends in the demand for skills. Examines shifts in the occupational and industrial distribution of jobs. Identifies the main factors that are changing skill demands. Presents evidence from employees on their perceptions of skill change.

| | |
|---|---|
| **- Empirical evidence on the nature of change in jobs and skills** | **36** |
| - Shift from manual to non-manual jobs | 36 |
| - Changing composition of intermediate level jobs | 38 |
| - Growth in professional jobs | 40 |
| - Employment remains significant in low-skill jobs | 40 |
| | |
| **- Overall increase in skill needs** | **41** |
| | |
| **- Why are skill needs changing?** | **43** |
| - Changing skill needs and new technology | 43 |
| - Skills needs and changing work organisation | 45 |
| | |
| **- Trends in demand for specific skills** | **46** |
| - Communication skills | 47 |
| - Cognitive skills and greater autonomy | 48 |
| - IT and new technology skills | 49 |
| - Management skills | 50 |
| - Standardisation and de-skilling | 53 |
| | |
| **- Summary** | **54** |

Chapter 4
## Qualifications of the workforce and job related skills ........................................ **59**

Examines trends in the supply of skills as proxied by qualifications. Looks at growth in participation and attainment in learning, particularly by young people. Maps out the trends in adult participation in training.

| | |
|---|---|
| **- The relationship between skills and qualifications** | **60** |
| - Rising qualification levels in the labour force | 61 |
| - Gaps in vocational attainment and at the intermediate level | 61 |
| - The long tail of low qualifications and the high incidence of poor basic skills | 63 |
| - Increased participation and attainment in general education | 65 |
| - Higher attainment at Levels 2 & 3 but limited growth in vocationally qualified | 66 |
| - Sharp growth in Higher Education | 68 |
| - Expansion in "new" vocational subjects | 69 |
| - Decline in traditional technical disciplines | 70 |
| - Dispersion of graduates through the labour market | 71 |

- Growth in incidence of training     **72**
    - Training provision skewed to the most able     73
    - Part-time/temporary workers     74
    - Small firms least likely to train     75
    - Much training is short term     76

- **The future supply of qualifications**     **77**

- **Summary**     **77**

## Chapter 5

## The balance between skills supply and demand: skill-related recruitment difficulties ............................................................. **85**

Presents evidence on the extent and nature of recruitment difficulties and external skills shortages experienced by employers. Looks at the impact of external skill shortages on firm performance.

- **'Skills shortages': Definitional Issues**     **86**

- **External skill shortages**     **87**
    - Trends over time in recruitment difficulties     87
    - Recent evidence on recruitment difficulties     89
    - Skills sought for hard-to-fill vacancies     93
    - The commercial impact of external skill shortages     95

- **Summary**     **98**

## Chapter 6

## Internal skills gaps and future skill requirements ................................... **100**

Examines the extent and nature of internal skill gaps being experienced by employers. Also looks at employers future business strategies to assess whether they are likely to experience future skill problems in pursuit of those strategies.

- **Internal skill gaps**     **100**
    - Employer perceptions of current skill deficiencies     100
    - Causes of skill gaps     107
    - The commercial impact of internal skill gaps     109
    - Are skill problems under-reported?     112
    - Forward-looking business strategies and future skill imbalances     113
    - Product strategies and skills gaps     115
    - Skills needed for higher-quality product strategies     116

- **Summary**     **120**

## Chapter 7

### Market signals - what earnings and the nature of unemployment tell us about where skills are needed 122

Presents evidence based on studies examining the returns to different qualifications and considers the implications for skills investment. Examines trends in wages and unemployment rates for different occupational groups as measures of the relative demand for particular skills.

- **The rate of return to skills** — 123
    - Returns to academic and vocational qualifications — 123
    - Returns to different levels of academic and vocational qualification — 124
    - Basic skills — 125
    - Generic skills — 126

- **Wage differentials between various skills** — 127
    - Manual Vs non-manual earnings — 127
    - Managers — 129
    - Professional occupations — 129
    - Intermediate jobs — 132
    - Lower skilled jobs — 133

- **Unemployment & skills** — 133

- **Summary** — 134

## Chapter 8

### Skill priorities 137

Concludes the report by describing the six main skill priority areas which the evidence suggests most warrant further investment.

- **Basic skills** — 138
- **Generic skills (including IT)** — 139
- **Intermediate level skills** — 140
- **Information and communication technology specialist skills** — 141
- **Mathematics** — 142
- **Major adult skills gaps** — 142

### Annexes

**Annex 1: Allocating qualifications to NVQ Level, (UK)** — 79

**Annex 2: Allocating qualifications to NVQ Level, (international comparisons)** — 82

**Annex A: Skills Task Force members** — 144

**Annex B: Skills Task Force Research Group members** — 145

# Figures

Figure 1    Occupational changes 1998 - 2009                                                    12

Figure 2a   Qualifications held at Level 2 by different age groups                               13

Figure 2b   Qualifications held at Level 3 by different age groups                               13

Figure 2.1  Productivity index - output per worker  1998 (UK=100)                               26

Figure 4.1  Qualification levels of economically active people of working age (UK)              61

Figure 4.2  Percentage of adult population aged 16 - 65 at document literacy level 1994/95      64

Figure 4.3  Percentage of pupils aged 15 in schools achieving 5 or more GCSEs A* - C,
            England 1988/89 to 1998/99                                                          65

Figure 4.4  Participation by young people in Higher Education, Age Participation Index (API),
            Great Britain, 1984/85 to 1998/99                                                   68

Figure 4.5  Employees receiving job-related training by highest qualification                   74

Figure 5.1  Skilled labour constraints on output in manufacturing companies and
            unemployed as a percent of total workforce, 1967-99                                 88

Figure 5.2  Total external skill shortages by occupation                                        91

Figure 5.3  Total external skill shortages by sector                                            92

Figure 5.4  Skills sought in connection with external skill shortages                           93

Figure 5.5  Impact of external skill shortages on establishment performance                     96

Figure 6.1  Skills sought in connection with internal skill gaps                               104

Figure 6.2  Main causes of international skills gaps cited by establishments
            with internal skills gaps                                                          107

Figure 6.3  Main impacts of internal skill gaps cited by establishments with internal skills gaps  110

Figure 6.4  Current skill proficiency and anticipated future problems arising from
            skill shortcomings                                                                 113

Figure 6.5  Anticipated commercial problems due to future skill shortcomings, analysed by
            recent change in sales                                                             114

Figure 6.6  New or additional skills required to move into higher quality product or service areas  117

Figure 6.7  Constraints on moving to higher value added product areas, analysed
            by recent change in sales                                                          119

Figure 7.1  Index of average male manual and non-manual earnings relative to
            the average male earnings                                                          128

Figure 7.2  Index of average female manual and non-manual earnings relative to
            average female earnings                                                            128

## Tables

Table 3.1    Employment trends by occupation 1971 - 1998 and projections for 2009, UK    37

Table 3.2    Employment by industry 1971 - 1998 and projections for 2004 and 2009, UK    37

Table 3.3    Employee perceptions of skill change    43

Table 3.4    Type of work skill changes in Britain 1992 - 1997    47

Table 3.5    Extent of use of management practices in UK in 1996    51

Table 3.6    Year of introduction of practices    51

Table 4.1    Trends in types and levels of qualifications held by those in employment (UK)    62

Table 4.2    Comparisons of qualifications at Level 2+ and 3+ in the UK, France and Germany    63

Table 4.3    Higher Education first degree attainment in selected subjects
in 1998 and change since 1994/95    69

Table 4.4    Number of registrations by subject area on HNC and HND courses
1989/90 to 1998/9    70

Table 4.5    Graduate penetration by occupation    72

Table 4.6    Employees receiving job-related training, by occupation and terms of employment    75

Table 5.1    Unfilled vacancies reported to Employment Service and estimated total vacancies
and external skill shortages in England, analysed by occupation category    89

Table 5.2    Total employment and estimated total vacancies, hard to fill vacancies and
external skill shortages in England, analysed by sector    91

Table 5.3    Distribution of external skill shortages by occupational area and sector    92

Table 5.4    Main skills sought in connection with external skill shortages,
analysed by occupational area    94

Table 5.5    Type of skills sought by establishments reporting external skill shortages    95

Table 5.6    Main impacts of external skill shortages on establishment performance    97

Table 6.1    Employee proficiency levels in current jobs, analysed by occupation    101

Table 6.2    Incidence of internal skill gaps, analysed by employee size-group and sector    102

Table 6.3    Private sector establishments analysed by incidence of skill problems and
changes in sales in previous 12 months    103

Table 6.4    Type of skills sought by establishments reporting internal skill gaps    105

Table 6.5    Main skills sought in connection with external skill shortages,
analysed by occupational area    106

Table 6.6    Main reasons for lack of full proficiency among existing staff,
analysed by occupational area    108

Table 6.7    Main impacts of lack of full proficiency on establishment performance,
analysed by occupational area    111

Table 6.8    Plans to move into higher product/service areas, analysed by recent change in sales    116

Table 6.9    Types of new or additional skills required to move into higher quality
product or service areas    116

Table 7.1    Index of male earnings by sub-major occupational group relative to SOC9.2    130

Table 7.2    Index of female earnings by sub-major occupational group relative to SOC9.2    131

Table 7.3    ILO Unemployment rates by broad occupational grouping (1979, 1990, 1999)    134

Table 7.4    ILO Unemployment rates by broad occupational grouping (1979, 1990, 1999)    134

# SKILLS TASK FORCE RESEARCH PAPER
## EXECUTIVE SUMMARY

## Introduction

* This report describes in more detail the research evidence which underpins the conclusions in the final report from the Skills Task Force as to where the UK's main skills gaps and shortages are to be found.

* The overall purpose has been to provide advice on the priority skill areas to which resources should be directed.

* The analysis is based on a wide range of research and analysis, much of it new and specifically commissioned for the Skills Task Force.

## What is meant by skill and why they are important

* At the core of the Task Force's understanding of the term skills is the idea of competence or proficiency - the ability to do something well. To some extent skills are hierarchical and the place of a skill in the hierarchy is substantially determined by the degree of complexity and discretion involved. Skills are also closely related to knowledge about the workings and capabilities of equipment, the product, processes and how different stages of production fit together.

* There are three main types of skills:

  * **Generic skills** - transferable employability skills used across a large number of different occupations

  * **Vocational skills** - occupational or technical skills needed to work within an occupation or occupational group

  * **Personal attributes** - the characteristics employers say they most often look for in an applicant when recruiting (e.g. motivation, judgement, leadership)

  * Higher levels of skill benefit the individual, the firm and the economy. Higher skilled individuals earn more, are less likely to be unemployed and live longer. Higher skills, used effectively, raise productivity in firms. Countries with a preponderance of higher skilled people tend to have higher economic growth.

# Changes in the nature of jobs and skills and levels of qualification

- There has been a broad shift in skill demand over the last 30 years away from skills related to manual work towards skills related to cognitive abilities. The shift in employment away from manual jobs towards non-manual jobs is a clear sign of this trend.

**Figure 1: Occupational changes 1998 - 2009**

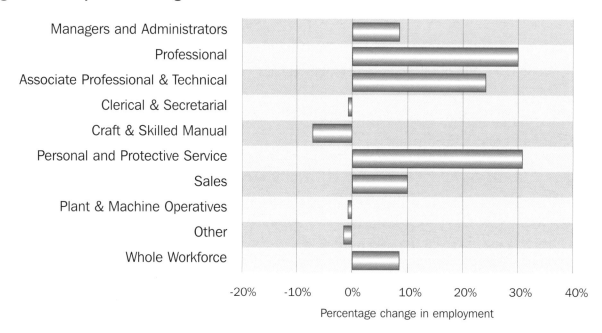

Percentage change in employment

- Generic skills (e.g. communication, problem solving and the ability to use IT equipment) are rising in demand. This is not to the exclusion of technical skills. Technical skills, for example those needed in most professional and skilled-trade jobs, are still vital to many companies. Technical skill demands in skilled-trade jobs are high because of the large retirement rate from these jobs.

- One of the most important shifts in jobs has occurred at the intermediate level where employment has moved away from traditional skilled-trade jobs towards associate professional ones. The skills needed in these "new" jobs are diverse but focus on creativity and design and the ability to translate ideas into a saleable product.

- New technology and global competition are both driving up skill demands. The precise impact of these developments on skills very much depends on how employers organise work and make use of new technologies. The trend is for new technologies, particularly IT, to lead to a greater demand for workers who can solve problems and interpret information. New work practices are leading to a rising demand for teamworking skills.

- The qualification level of the workforce has risen significantly over the last 20 years fuelled mainly by higher qualifications gained by new entrants to the labour market. The proportion of young people gaining 5+ GCSEs, 2+ GCE A-levels and acquiring degrees have all risen substantially since the late 1980s.

- There has been little growth in the qualification levels of the existing (adult) workforce. Furthermore the growth in qualifications gained by young people has favoured academic qualifications. Most of the growth in young people gaining vocational qualifications has been at low levels (below NVQ Level 3).

- Consequently:

  - A large minority of the UK workforce still have either low or no qualifications

  - The UK still falls a long way short of its main competitors in terms of the proportion of the labour force holding vocational qualifications at Levels 2 and 3

  - Around one fifth of adults have poor basic skills

**Figure 2a: Qualifications held at Level 2 by different age groups**

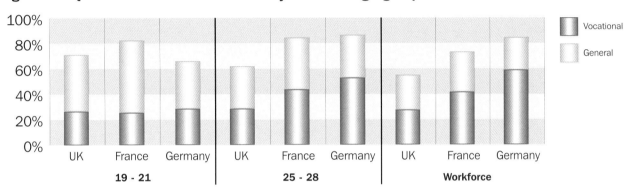

**Figure 2b: Qualifications held at Level 3 by different age groups**

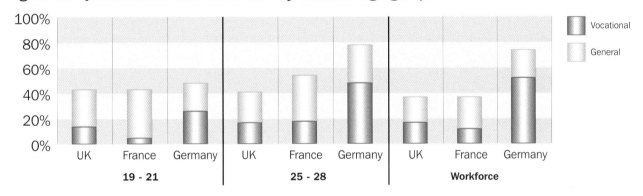

Source: Updating the Skills Audit data 1998 (2000) - unpublished
(1) Aged 16-64 (UK women aged 16-59)
(2) Former Bundesrepublik (FRG)
Note: the figures for Germany are for 1997.

- In terms of specific skills the UK produces a limited pool of young people with a good level of ability in technical subjects such as maths and physics. Not only does this mean that the overall numbers able to take up further study and careers in technical disciplines are limited but that few of the most able are qualified in these areas.

## Mismatches in skill supply and demand

- Skills shortages are concentrated in technical jobs - 4 in 10 skill shortage vacancies found in The Employers' Skill Survey (ESS) in autumn 1999 were in craft or associate professional jobs. Sales jobs were the next most likely occupation to suffer from skill shortages (13% of skill shortage vacancies).

- Employers unable to find appropriately skilled individuals to fill craft and associate professional jobs are looking for particular types of technical skills and not only generic skills.

- Wage differentials are lower for craft and technical level jobs than for those at professional and managerial level.  However, the rate of return to gaining intermediate level technical (vocational) qualifications is comparable to that for academic qualifications - when allowance is made for the shorter time needed to acquire vocational qualifications.

- Skill gaps among existing employees were recognised by about one in five employers in ESS. Skill gaps are more likely to be reported in less-skilled occupations such as sales, personal service and operative and assembly operations.  The majority of establishments with skill gaps said their employees lacked a mix of generic and vocational skills.

- The least skilled have the most limited opportunities in the labour market reflecting a mismatch between the skills they have and those demanded by the labour market.  The relative rate of unemployment for the least skilled has increased over the last 20 years.  The least qualified have seen their earnings worsen considerably relative to the better qualified.

- The Employers case study research suggests that many current skill gaps pass unrecognised by employers and that the one-fifth of employers reporting a skills gap in ESS is likely to be an under-estimate.

- Employers are more likely to perceive a skills gap in their existing workforce when they consider how they will deal with future commercial problems.  Almost half of employers in ESS anticipated that commercial problems would arise in the next two or three years as a result of shortfalls in the skills of existing employees.

## Skill priorities

- **Basic skills** - those of literacy and numeracy, the basic building blocks on which to build other skills.  Seven million adults in England - one in five - are functionally illiterate.  Problems with numeracy skills are believed to be even worse.  People who lack these skills are less likely to find work and where they do they earn well below average earnings.  Individuals with poor basic skills can act as a brake on the performance of companies.

- **Generic skills** - transferable employability skills used across a large number of different occupations.  These skills are needed in all jobs and demand for them has increased as the nature of employment has changed.  The generic skills most in demand are those of communication, teamworking and problem solving.

- **Mathematics skills** - competence in mathematics significantly above basic numeracy. The ability to work with numbers and solve problems using mathematical concepts and methods is valued in the labour market - a young adult with a GCE A-level earns significantly more than one with only GCSE maths. Despite this only 45% of young people gain a GCSE grade C in maths at 15, only 10% of the cohort gain GCE A-level mathematics and only just over 1% of those gaining a first degree in 1998 gained one in mathematics.

- **Intermediate level skills** - specific occupational skills needed in intermediate jobs ranging from craft to associate professional occupations. ESS found that 48% of all skill shortage vacancies were in these jobs. The German workforce has twice as many people with vocational qualifications at Level 2 than the UK and three time as many with vocational qualifications at Level 3.

- **Specialist information and communications technology skills** - professional skills needed in the ICT sector and by ICT specialists in other industries. While there has been strong growth in Higher Education provision in IT there are concerns about the abilities of some IT graduates. In particular, the extent to which the supply of people qualified in IT is keeping pace with demands not only in terms of quantity but also in terms of the mix of skills offered. The mean A-level score of new entrants to IT courses in Higher Education is 25% lower than the average for all courses. Employers report that individuals with good IT skills coupled with high levels of business awareness and generic skills are at a premium.

- **Major adult skill gaps** - the large proportion of the workforce with no qualifications or qualifications below Level 2. Despite the growth in qualifications held by the workforce, one-third of the adult workforce does not even hold a Level 2 qualification. The majority of those without qualifications are also those described above as lacking basic skills. Many are unwilling or don't recognise gaps in their skills and many have found ways of working around or disguising the problem.

# CHAPTER 1
## INTRODUCTION

**1.1** This report describes in more detail the research evidence which underpins the conclusions in the final report from the Skills Task Force as to where the UK's main skills gaps and skill shortages are to be found. The intention in publishing this report is not only to make the evidence considered by the Task Force available to public scrutiny, but also to stimulate further research and to offer a structure and method for making assessments of skills gaps and skills shortages in the future.

**1.2** In gathering the evidence for its work the Task Force has consulted widely. Consultation events have been held on the skills needed in a range of sectors and a series of research reports summarising the skill position in different sectors and occupations have been published. In addition the Task Force has commissioned the largest programme of research on skills ever undertaken. Reports from each element of this research programme will be published separately. Studies have included:

- a telephone survey of 23,000 employers and a face-to-face survey of 4,000 employers focusing on the incidence, scale and commercial impact of the skill problems they faced in autumn 1999 (hereafter termed the Employers' Skill Survey);

- case studies of seven different industries (banking and finance, telecommunications, hotels, food processing, engineering, health and social care and local and central government) investigating in more detail how skills affect the products and services companies produce and offer and the ways they manufacture or deliver them (hereafter termed the Employer Case Studies);

- projections of employment by occupation and qualification through to 2009;

- estimates of the returns and rates of return to Level 2 and 3 vocational qualifications and basic skills;

- updated comparisons of the proportion of young people and the workforce in the UK, France and Germany with qualifications at Levels 2 and 3; and

- international comparisons of students entering Higher Education courses in engineering and computer science (phase 1).

**1.3** This chapter goes on to outline the approach taken in considering the evidence and producing the report. Chapter 2 defines the terms used throughout the report and, in particular, sets out the way the term 'skill' is used in the report. Chapter 3 discusses the demand for skills both in terms of recent historical trends and future projections. Chapter 4 provides a similar analysis for supply though it is obliged by data constraints to focus mainly on trends in qualifications as a proxy for skills. Chapters 5, 6 and 7 provide the main analyses on whether demand and supply are in balance. Chapter 5 outlines the evidence derived from employers' perceptions of their external recruitment difficulties, and Chapter 6 the evidence on their perceptions of internal skills gaps and prospective future skill shortcomings which could hamper business performance. Chapter 7 focuses on the main market signals about the extent to which skill needs are being met - relative earnings and relative returns to different levels and types of skills (again mainly using qualifications as a proxy for skills). Chapter 8 presents conclusions regarding the skill priority areas in which the evidence presented in this paper suggests further investment in skills would be most beneficial.

## Our approach

1.4 The basic analytical approach is the one familiar to economists. It is to analyse the supply and demand for skills, to compare the two and identify areas of mismatch. Unfortunately it has not been possible to look at the supply and demand for skills directly because of the absence of direct measures. Instead the analysis most usually relies on proxies for skills such as qualifications and the occupational level of the job, though the report does refer to some research that aims at more direct measures.

1.5 The main aim is to identify key skill priority areas for future investment. The problem is how to identify what those skill priority areas are. What evidence would signal where further investment is needed? What criteria should be used to determine that further public funding is needed in a particular skill area?

## Analyses based on rates of return

1.6 The best evidence would be that which demonstrated the skills with the highest rate of return. Further investment in these skills would be most beneficial to the economy. This ideal measure would be the marginal return to particular skills in the widest sense (the social rate of return) and would also refer to the prospective rather than retrospective rate of return. This would give the best assessment of the benefit of additional skills in a particular area measured in terms of the costs and benefits to individuals and society as a whole. However, there is little research which has managed to match this ideal and much further work is needed before practical measures can be produced which approximate to it.

1.7 Measuring the wider or social rate of return to a particular skill is very problematic. Much research, particularly that related to the UK, is based on private rates of return. Focusing on private rates of return ignores the wider benefits from education and training. It understates the overall rate of return to skill acquisition, leaving out some of the major benefits that are sought through publicly funded education and training - e.g. greater wealth for the exchequer (in terms of more taxes and fewer benefit recipients), spin-off benefits from higher productivity from lower skilled workers working with higher skilled co-workers and reductions in the crime rate.

1.8 Nevertheless, where the financial return to an individual from acquiring a certain type or level of skill greatly exceeds the costs of acquiring that skill (in terms of the direct and opportunity costs of the learning), this could signify a shortage in that particular skill area. This is a very useful method for identifying where employers are prepared to offer wage premia for skills they need and this method of analysis is used to help identify general trends in skill requirements in the report. However, the wages employers offer are affected by a wide range of factors and do not exclusively reflect the skill levels of employees. For example, pay differentials agreed under collective agreements may act as barriers to employers offering a higher level of pay for certain kinds of skill, even though demand for those skills is strong. Increased flexibility within the labour market in recent years may have reduced this problem but it still exists.

**1.9** Rates of return research which does exist makes it difficult to define what an 'excessive' rate of return to a particular type or level of skill may be. One way to do this would be to examine trends in the rate of return over time as well as their absolute levels. One can then define skill areas with the fastest growing and largest rates of return as those with the greatest likelihood of supply failing to keep up with demand. However, some of the other determinants of wages mentioned above can also cause changes in rates of return. For example, changes in rates of return might reflect changes in bargaining power, changing working conditions or social acceptance that we need to pay more for certain skills (the report refers to increases in relative pay for managers as an example of this).

**1.10** Most rates of return analyses tend to focus on skills, or rather qualifications, at a broad level (e.g. at best the level of qualification achieved or numbers of years of education). As such they do not say much if anything about the demand for specific kinds of skill. Furthermore, analyses are based on current structures (e.g. where qualification level is used as a proxy for skill, they are based on current qualification structures) and they do not tell us what returns would be under different structures. This, therefore, limits the usefulness of these findings when talking about future skills needs within a different structural framework.

## Trends in jobs and earnings

**1.11** For these reasons the analyses in this report are broadly based and embrace several different approaches. In addition to considering rates of return, the report also draws on extensive data from the New Earnings Survey and Labour Force Survey on trends in earnings at a fairly detailed level. This gives an insight into those occupations where wages have been rising fastest which could indicate the areas where skill shortages are most prevalent. As with the rates of return analysis, we have to remember that many employers claim they do not respond to skill shortages by raising wages.[1]

**1.12** Trends in the occupational and industrial mix of the workforce also provide indications of potential mismatches between skills supply and demand. Occupations experiencing particularly rapid growth may well be those in which employers have greatest difficulty in finding appropriately skilled staff. Furthermore, as occupational groups are loosely based around common skill sets, an analysis of this type of data does provide some guide as to which types of skills are in increasing demand and which types of skills are no longer needed in the labour market. As a large amount of data over time exists on this basis, and a good understanding of the factors that are driving employment trends by occupation and industry is also available, we can produce forecasts of changes over the next 10-15 years with reasonable accuracy. These provide a forward-looking element to the analysis though it is accepted that trends in occupations serve merely as a proxy for skills.

## Trends in skills supply

**1.13** As the purpose of the analysis is to compare trends in the demand for skill with trends in the supply, extensive use is made of information on participation in education and training, together with the acquisition of qualifications, as a means to better understand supply. Much information is available on participation and achievement by level and subject. This can be compared to the type and level of jobs available in the labour market. However, it

---

[1] Only half the employers saying that they were suffering from external skill shortages in the Employers' Skills Survey said they raise wages as a result.

is recognised that many courses are not designed to prepare people for a specific job in the labour market, and that there are severe limits to this type of analysis - though broad trends in more vocationally-orientated subjects (e.g. engineering) are very helpful. In addition, the major discontinuities in much of the subject data on participation and qualifications are a significant problem, as is the fragmented nature of much of the data (it tends to be organised by provider). It is also important to recognise that, as with the analyses of occupations, the report uses proxies for skills - qualifications and courses in this instance.

## Direct measures of skills and employer-based research

1.14 Recent research has attempted to circumvent the use of proxy measures of skill by devising ways of directly measuring skills. There are standard tests which can be used in surveys to measure people's basic skills. In the UK, other research uses individuals' perceptions of the skills they need and asks respondents views on how these have changed over time. The subjective nature of this research can be criticised. On the other hand findings from the research in terms of relative skill levels do conform with what we would expect (see Paragraph 3.25 below) and the measures do appear to be relatively robust. This research provides some of the best evidence we have on changes in the demand for specific types of skill.

1.15 Another common way of trying to judge which skills are in shortest supply in the economy is to ask employers where problems lie. There are several regular surveys which ask employers various questions about problems in recruiting people and about skill deficiencies among their existing employees. The report supplements these surveys with the Task Force's extensive employer-based study on trends in recruitment difficulties and skill deficiencies.

1.16 While providing useful data on the trend in skill problems and some pointers about where the problems lie, these types of surveys have some inherent weaknesses. It is very difficult to devise appropriate questions to identify the extent to which employer difficulties in recruiting people and running their business are due to skill problems. There may be other reasons why employers are unable to recruit (unattractive job, poor recruitment practices) and it is very difficult, for employers and other analysts, to assess the link between skills and business performance. For these reasons findings from these types of surveys can be difficult to interpret.

1.17 On top of this there are issues around whether employers are fully aware of their skill needs. The Task Force's research suggests that skills tend to be a neglected issue when employers are formulating their business strategies. There must be a question therefore about whether employers properly evaluate their skill needs and, even where they do attempt to do so, whether they give full consideration to these needs before they embark on a particular product strategy. If they fail to do this - and the evidence from case studies is that many who do so fail - we would expect to find instances where employers do not have the skills needed to meet their business objectives or where business objectives are set relatively low because of poor knowledge about the availability of skills.

**1.18** One way to better understand the extent to which employers have skill deficiencies among their workforce is to compare firms of similar size in similar product markets, looking at the extent to which differences in performance are related to differences in skill levels. This was the approach taken in the studies carried out by the National Institute of Economic and Social Research (NIESR) in the mid/late 1980s and early 1990s when matched samples of firms in the UK and other countries were compared in order to assess the extent to which lower productivity in UK firms was related to a lower level of skill in the workforce. These studies are referred to in the report. However, they are now becoming a little dated and the Task Force has undertaken their own case studies of firms in the UK (time and resources would not allow comparisons with firms from other countries) to assess the relationship between firm performance and skills. As with all case studies the findings are not applicable to the population at large, though some efforts to deal with this problem have been made by selecting case studies across a range of firms within a given sector. The case studies undertaken on behalf of the Task Force have also been supplemented by a large-scale representative telephone and face-to-face survey.

**1.19** The approach taken in this report is therefore an eclectic one. It considers the range of evidence available to form a judgment on where the skill needs of the economy seem to be most pressing and to address the following questions: What are the main skills in demand? How will they change in the future? Looking at the outputs from the various institutions developing skills, what are the overall trends in supply? What is likely to change in the future? What kinds of mismatch between skills supply and demand are most likely to occur in the future?

# CHAPTER 2
## WHAT WE MEAN BY SKILL AND WHY SKILLS ARE IMPORTANT

## Introduction

**2.1**   The concept of skill is difficult to define and there are many different perspectives and nuances. The purpose of this chapter is to set out the concept of the term skill used through the paper and define the terms for different aspects of skill.

**2.2**   Most commentators accept that there are different levels and types of skills. However, problems arise over the definition of the different levels and the factors that determine this, and the definition of different types of skills. The remit for this paper did not extend to contributing to this debate - the main aim of the paper is to provide empirical evidence on the range of skills needed and available in the economy. In order to ensure clarity, we present a set of working definitions for the concept of skill most relevant to the analysis provided in this paper. It is accepted that others may have chosen to emphasise different aspects of the term skill.

**2.3**   There is also some debate over the contribution of skills to economic competitiveness and social well-being. This report assumes that high skill levels are crucial to both. We cannot have a competitive economy without having the skills necessary to achieve high levels of productivity. In the long run, the most profitable firms will be those providing the highest value-added. Much of that added value will come from a competitive edge in terms of the quality of the workforce. Skills are an important pre-requisite for innovation and technological advancement. Individuals are most likely to earn more and have more rewarding jobs and lives if they have a high level of skill. They are more likely to be able to cope with change. This chapter reviews the evidence that leads to these conclusions.

## Skills - definitions & conceptual issues

### Skills hierarchies

**2.4**   At the core of the term skill is the idea of competence or proficiency - the ability to do something well. Skill is the ability to perform a task to a pre-defined standard of competence, but to many the word also connotes a dimension of increasing ability (i.e. a hierarchy of skill). Thus while skill is synonymous with competence, it also evokes images of expertise, mastery and excellence. Skill is by definition acquired through formal and/or informal learning and through practice.

**2.5**   An individual is unlikely to be able to do something well if he or she does not have a good grasp of the processes involved and how they work. Skills therefore go hand in hand with knowledge. Some skills can be performed without a good level of underpinning knowledge and understanding. However, to apply skills in a wide range of contexts and situations demands a fundamental level of knowledge related to that skill.

**2.6** The Task Force said in its first report that it aimed to establish a "national culture of high skills". It should have perhaps specified a high level of knowledge as part of this. It also emphasised its desire to see a UK economy where skills are pervasive when it said in its second report that it had a "vision of a society in which skill is widespread". What did the Task Force mean by this?

**2.7** Economies based on high levels of skill and knowledge could produce two different outcomes. A high level of national wealth may be produced where that wealth derives from many, but not all, workers possessing high levels of skill. Alternatively high levels of skill and knowledge may predominate throughout the economy. The Task Force's vision is closer to the second model. It is this model where in economic terms labour productivity is likely to be maximised and where in social terms all can contribute to and benefit from national wealth.

**2.8** Skills and knowledge are attributes of a person or requirements of a job. Some jobs make greater demands than others and some people are more skilled than others. The Task Force wants to ensure that the UK has as many high skilled jobs and highly skilled people as possible.

**Complexity and discretion**

**2.9** Much of the literature highlights two dimensions of work which largely determine the place of a job or person in the skills hierarchy, namely its complexity and the amount of discretion required to operate effectively.

**2.10** Complexity varies according to the techniques, dexterity, simplicity or complexity of procedures and the number and range of tasks involved. It also depends on the knowledge needed about the workings and capabilities of equipment, the product, processes, and how different stages fit together.

**2.11** Discretion refers to the element of choice and potential to exercise judgement. All jobs operate within "prescribed" sets of rules, regulations, custom and practice which limit discretion in varying degrees. All jobs consist of a mix of choice/judgement and prescription and the degree of skill depends on the balance - the greater the share of choice/judgement required to carry out a particular function the higher the skill is ranked in the overall skill hierarchy.

**2.12** These concepts of complexity and discretion are important in considering the changing skill needs of the economy. The report refers to them on a number of occasions in explaining why some jobs are more skilled than others and why the general skill requirements of the economy are increasing. They are also important in understanding the on-going debate about the degree of upskilling and de-skilling in jobs.

**Cognitive and manual skills**

**2.13** A further dimension of skill which is relevant to the place of a job or person in the skills hierarchy is the extent to which performance of tasks primarily involves thinking, reasoning and the use of knowledge or whether it mainly relies on hand/eye co-ordination and physical attributes. These two different kinds of skill sets will be referred to as cognitive and manual skills respectively. There is a perception in the common understanding of skill that jobs or tasks requiring a significant cognitive input are higher skilled than those requiring a greater degree of manual input. This leads to a widely held view that the move from blue-collar manual jobs to white-collar employment in the economy generally reflects a move up the skills hierarchy as white-collar jobs are assumed to place a greater emphasis on cognitive skills than blue-collar jobs.

2.14 However, a growing number of jobs require a combination of cognitive and manual skills in both the service and the industrial sectors of the economy. Hence, it is not possible to make a clear and simple distinction between manual and non-manual and higher and lower level skills and jobs. There are many manual jobs which require a relatively high level of skill - for example, those used in many craft and technical jobs. Conversely there are non-manual jobs which require a relative low level of skill - for example those used in some clerical and personal service jobs.

**Economic worth of skills and their application to jobs**

2.15 Skill levels are not only defined by the degree of complexity and discretion or cognitive and manual skills they involve. They also tend to be defined in terms of their relative economic worth and their importance to the firm, which in turn depends on the relative demand and level of learning needed to acquire a particular skill.

2.16 The relative demand for a skill is likely to be affected by such things as technology and social norms and as such the economic value of skills changes over time. For example, the ability to repair a mechanical typewriter (involving as it did significant diagnostic skills and understanding of the machines) would have been considered a valuable technical skill in the first half of the twentieth century. Today, many of these skills have been rendered redundant by the word-processor. While skills persist as attributes acquired by individuals, the value of these skills change over time in response to changes in the market.

2.17 Skills that take a long time to acquire will, other things being equal, tend to attract higher rewards. This serves as both an incentive to invest in learning and reflects the higher added value of the skills acquired. So, for example, barristers earn much more than hairdressers because they have invested longer in acquiring their skills and those skills have a higher valuation in the market place.

2.18 Jobs seldom require just one skill. They usually demand a range of skills. It is the relative weight of the different skills a job needs that often determines its place in the skills hierarchy. It is also important to note that the range of skills needed in a job changes over time. Some skills become less important or redundant while others become more important or new skills are needed in a particular job. The balance between retention of existing skills and development of new skills is the key to understanding how skill needs are changing within jobs.

**Generic/vocational skills and personal attributes**

**2.19** In summary, skills can be ranked in a hierarchy determined by degrees of autonomy; there are different dimensions of skills (cognitive, manual) and most jobs require more than the exercise of one skill on one or more dimensions. We now propose a slightly different definition of skill types than that advanced in the Task Force's first report. Skills can be either "generic" or "vocational" (though with different degrees of transferability) and there is a third group of "skills" better defined as personal attributes such as the ability to interact well with other people or to motivate oneself and others.

**2.20 Generic skills** are those skills which can be used across large numbers of different occupations. They include what are defined as the Key Skills - communication, problem solving, team working, IT skills, application of number and an ability to improve personal learning and performance. They also include reasoning skills, scheduling work and diagnosing work problems, work process management skills, visualising output, working backwards for planning purposes, and sequencing operations. The demand for these skills has increased in recent years, fuelled by the increased emphasis on satisfying customers and the growing complexity and autonomy of many jobs.

**2.21 Vocational skills** are occupational or technical skills needed to work within an occupation or occupational group. They are essential for undertaking certain job tasks. Some vocational skills (e.g. foreign language skills, computer programming skills) are transferable across <u>some</u> occupations while others (e.g. operating particular pieces of machinery) are not. A common trend is for people to have a primary occupational skill, such as a mechanical engineer, which is enhanced through the development of dual or multi-skilling in another, related, occupational area, such as electrical engineering.

**2.22 Personal attributes** are more difficult to define and many have argued they are not skills at all (Keep & Mayhew, 1999). They relate to the characteristics that employers say they most often look for in an applicant when recruiting. They are frequently defined in terms of motivation, judgement, leadership and initiative. Some can be taught or learned (e.g. leadership) while others are more immutable, though not to the extent that they cannot be improved through some form of learning. Personal attributes encapsulate the desire of employers for employees who are flexible, adaptable, and able to cope with change and uncertainty. Employers' greater use of aptitude testing and assessment centres testify to the increasing importance of these attributes in developing a workforce that is well suited to the needs of a high growth economy.

## Skill formation

**2.23** Skills can be acquired through a number of different ways or, as commonly described, routes. Full-time education's main role is to provide individuals with a core level of basic, generic and some technical and practical skills which can be built on throughout their working life. The Task Force stressed in its earlier reports the importance of individuals acquiring a good level of mathematical ability by the end of full-time education. There is also a role for the formal education system in socialising individuals to understand how important inter-personal skills, other generic skills and attributes such as high motivation are for success in the labour market and adult life.

**2.24** Vocational education and training places a greater emphasis on acquiring practical skills needed in particular occupations or specific jobs. Clearly full-time education can play a role here in that many full-time courses are of a vocational nature, particularly in further and higher education. A significant part of this practical skills formation is better suited to learning in the workplace, either through learning on-the-job or off-the-job, learning that can be practised and reinforced in a work environment. Work experience within a full-time education context also has a role to play in developing these skills.

**2.25** Work-based learning also has an important role in developing more generic skills and some personal attributes. We have said above that full-time education also needs to provide a similar contribution to this type of skill formation. However, there are some generic skills such as team working and business awareness, and attributes such as leadership and judgement, which are linked to maturity and experience. In this respect work-based learning will always play an essential role in bringing individuals up to their full potential.

**2.26** It is very important that skill formation is developed in a balanced manner. To have an effective workforce we need individuals who are adaptable and able to apply and build on their skills in a range of contexts to meet changing labour market needs. The economy needs individuals with a good mix of technical and practical skills. The demand for this mix of skills was clearly apparent in the employers' survey which we refer to later in the report. Green (1998) has pointed to an historic absence of a strong element of general education within English vocational education and training. This has produced a weakness in parts of the workforce in terms of their ability to adapt their skills to technological and other changes. Similarly, the early specialisation of those most likely to form the higher skilled element of the workforce can be seen as unhelpful in developing the broader range of practical and generic skills needed for career advancement including supervisory and management roles.

## The role of skills

**2.27** The future prosperity of the country, our competitiveness and social well-being is linked to being able to produce a growing level of high value-added products and services. The Task Force stated in its earlier reports that high levels of productivity based on high levels of skill will form the basis for this type of economy. The productivity of the UK economy lags behind that of many of our competitors. As Figure 2.1 shows, productivity as measured by output per worker is 13% above the UK level in Germany, 21% higher in France and 36% higher in the US.

**2.28** Increasing skills in the UK could help to raise productivity growth and so help to reduce the size of this productivity gap. Even small changes in productivity can have a large impact on output. For example, if raising skills in the UK only increased productivity growth by 0.1 per cent a year the economy could generate somewhere in the region of £10 billion more output over the next ten years.

**Figure 2.1 Productivity index - output per worker 1998 (UK=100)**

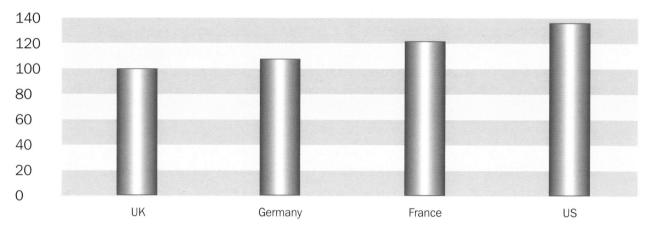

Source: OECD

**2.29** This does not mean that skills are the only factor in improving the UK's labour productivity and economic performance. The role skills play is a complex one. Research has shown that economic growth, and productivity in particular, is also related to the level of capital investment. There is a strong body of evidence that comparative investment in capital stock has been much lower in the UK than in our major international competitors since WWII (Crafts & O'Mahony 1999). As a result the capital intensity of the French economy is 40% higher than the UK, Germany 65% higher, Japan 50% higher and the US 30% higher (O'Mahony 1999). Investment in capital and skills are often complementary and their combined impact on economic growth can be greater than the sum of their individual contributions.

**2.30** Of course, the level of upskilling will not simply depend on the supply of skills from individuals but also on the utilisation of those skills by employers. The Task Force in its work has always assumed that in the long run it is in the best interests of the UK as a whole to compete in the high value-added, high skilled segment of markets. This is not to say that UK firms cannot compete on price in low added-value product markets that demand relatively low levels of skill and pay relatively low wages. Clearly many firms do compete very successfully in these product markets - particularly where international competition is low and where domestic demand for these types of goods and services is high. However, it is the Task Force's view that a UK economy that is over-reliant on this type of business is very vulnerable to global competition. It is also likely to produce a poorer society with lower living standards than the leading economies of the world.

### The benefits of skills to the individual

**2.31** An important benefit for a society with higher levels of skill is that individuals with higher levels of skill are more prosperous and have better labour market experiences (OECD, 1998). Many studies have demonstrated that earnings are positively correlated with education levels and, furthermore, that expanded education participation in western countries over many decades has not in general led to declining rates of return to education[1]. The evidence for the UK and other western economies suggest that on average the return to a year's additional education is between 5-10%[2]- though some estimates place the return considerably higher.[3]

---

[1] We recognise that the focus in these studies is on qualifications as a proxy for skills. We accept that this is only a limited proxy but there is good evidence to show a close correlation between qualification and skill levels.

[2] Dearden (1998) and Dearden (1999) warn that using an average rate or return based on additional years of full-time education is misleading particularly for those who undertook a lot of their post-school qualifications on a part-time basis. Annual rates of return are very heterogeneous and depend crucially on qualifications undertaken.

[3] Harmon and Walker (1995) found returns of 15%.

**2.32** There are significant differences depending on the type of qualification obtained. It is estimated that the return to completing a GCE A-level qualification (compared to those gaining just GCSEs) is $7^1/_2$-9% per annum for men and 9-11$^1/_2$% for women with comparable annual rates of returns for equivalent vocational qualifications (ONC/OND, C&G higher), at least for men. The annual premium related to a first degree over those with just GCE A-levels is in the range of 3-9% for men and 7-8% for women with again similar returns for equivalent vocational qualifications (HNC/HND) (Dearden et al (1999)).

**2.33** Individual benefits from education are cumulative in the sense that those with higher levels of education and qualifications are also those most likely to receive training while in work. The private returns to this training have consistently been found to be significant. Individuals undertaking employer-provided or vocational training earn on average just above 5% higher real earnings than individuals who have not undertaken such training (Blundell, Dearden and Meghir, 1996).

**2.34** Only a few studies such as Bishop (1994, 1997) have examined the direct impact of training on productivity at the individual level. On the basis of surveys of US employers which focus on each firm's most recently hired employee, Bishop (1997) is able to quantify the relationship between the time invested in on-the-job training of workers in different occupations and their reported growth in productivity over the following two years. In the service sector, retail sales, clerical and blue-collar workers who received more on-the-job training, achieved average productivity growth rates in the first three months of employment that were higher than in the next 21 months, but the reverse was true for the more highly trained managerial and professional employees. Formal on-the-job training received from a previous employer was found to significantly increase the initial productivity of newly-hired employees and reduce the time required for the new firm to train them (ibid).

**2.35** There are two main competing hypotheses which have been put forward to explain the relationship between earnings and qualifications. The first, with its roots in human capital theory, focuses on the ways in which education may enhance the economic value of individuals, for example, by increasing their ability to respond to new opportunities (Schultz, 1975). The second approach emphasises the ways that educational qualifications operate as screening devices for the personal attributes sought by employers (Spence, 1973). Both these hypotheses are consistent with available evidence and it is likely that formally-certified education serves both sets of purposes in varying degrees.

**2.36** However, in the last 15-20 years several western countries such as Britain and the US have experienced rapid growth in educational salary premia and widening disparities in income between low-skilled and university-educated individuals. The emphasis in labour market research has therefore tended to shift away from old arguments about whether education serves to enhance the economic value of individuals. The focus is now on identifying the main factors underpinning the apparent growth in demand for highly-educated employees. Much of this research points to the existence of important complementarities between high-level skills and the diffusion of advanced technologies, in particular, microelectronics-based equipment (Lloyd-Ellis, 1999), and is discussed further in Chapter 3.

## The benefits of skills to firms

2.37 The empirical evidence on the benefits of higher skill levels to firms is not as robust as that on the benefits to individuals, not least because it is difficult to measure the stock of skills within the firm. There are also problems in demonstrating a causal link between skills and productivity, competitiveness and profitability because of the impact of other intervening variables (e.g. the economic cycle, exchange rate, business restructuring). Nevertheless logic suggests employers invest in raising the skill levels of their workforce (through training) with the expectation of receiving a return on this investment in terms of higher productivity, competitiveness and profitability. We discussed above the evidence that employees who receive training gain financially as a result. We would expect that these higher wages are paid from firms' higher productivity and profitability resulting, at least in part, from the training investment.

2.38 Research tends to support these theoretical assumptions. Firms that invest in training, thereby raising the stock of skills available in the workplace, are more productive. This higher productivity seems to be particularly related to greater technical skills in the workforce which enables more flexibility in work practices and reduces waste through, for example, less equipment downtime. Firms that are less prone to skills problems are also those with higher levels of productivity.

2.39 Dearden, Reed and van Reenen (1999) have found that training significantly boosts productivity in the productive sector of the British economy. Raising the proportion of workers trained in an industry, and thereby the stock of available skills, from 10% (the mean) to 15% is associated with at least a 3% percentage point increase in the value added per worker. An OECD study found that training does generate increased wages for trained workers, and increased productivity for those enterprises that train and innovate (OECD, 1994).

2.40 Several recent US studies have sought to investigate the links between workforce skills and performance at the level of individual firms. Bartel (1994) finds that manufacturers which had lower productivity than comparable firms in their sector in 1983 were more likely to invest in training programmes that resulted in significantly higher levels of productivity growth in the subsequent three years, thus helping them to close the productivity gap. Black and Lynch (1996) found that simple measures of the number of workers receiving training at given points in time have no apparent effects on labour productivity in individual establishments. However, in manufacturing plants productivity is positively related to formal, off-the-job training while in service establishments training in computer skills is found to have a positive effect on productivity. There are also many studies which consider the impact of investments in training in the context of wider changes in work organisation: For example, Ichniowski, Shaw and Prennushi (1997) found that productivity levels in US steel plants are significantly higher on production lines where a cluster of innovative work practices, including higher levels of training, have been adopted.

2.41 A recent study of the returns to in-company training in Ireland has found a positive and statistically significant relationship between sales per employee and the provision of general training, that is, training in skills which may be useful in other firms (Barrett and O'Connell, 1998). However, there was no such relationship between sales per employee and the provision of firm-specific training. The authors conclude that the performance benefits arising from general training may have outweighed any increase in the tendency for employees in receipt of general training to move to other firms.

**2.42** In Britain, some studies focus on the other side of the coin, namely, the economic impact of shortages of skilled labour. Nickell and Nicolitsas (1999) panel data analysis of a large number of UK manufacturing companies suggests that difficulties in recruiting skilled labour may have cumulative and permanent effects on output through their depressive effects on complementary investments in physical capital. These results support an earlier study at the industry level by Haskel and Martin (1993) which found significant negative effects on labour productivity of recruitment difficulties for skilled labour. Some of the mechanisms by which such effects might occur include delays in the introduction of new technology and a slowdown in efficiency improvements deriving from on-the-job learning.

**2.43** A number of studies by researchers at the National Institute of Economic and Social research (NIESR) have investigated the link between skill levels and labour productivity by comparing matched samples of UK manufacturing firms and hotels with comparable Continental European counterparts. The studies found that the higher average levels of labour productivity in continental plants were closely related to greater technical skills and knowledge in their workforce. The higher productivity of Continental plants was related to the greater ability of shopfloor workers to perform a wide range of tasks leading to higher quality products and services, a reduction in downtime from machinery breakdown; and better front-line supervisory capabilities reducing the need for managers to be involved in day-to-day production decisions. Higher average skill levels were also related to the earlier introduction of new technologies. (Daly, Hitchens and Wagner, 1985; Mason and van Ark, 1994 - engineering; Steedman and Wagner, 1987 - wood furniture; Steedman and Wagner, 1989 - clothing manufacture; Mason, van Ark and Wagner, 1994 - food manufacture; Prais, Jarvis and Wagner, 1989, hotels).

**2.44** While the Anglo-German comparisons have focussed attention on cross-country differences in intermediate (craft- and technician-level) skills, other comparisons involving the US have shown how mass higher education can also have a favourable effect on productivity, for example, by providing the graduate engineers needed to design and manage large-scale production processes (Mason and Finegold, 1997).

**2.45** While these studies demonstrated that higher skills raised firm productivity, they did not demonstrate that they raised firm profitability. As noted earlier, firms can still remain profitable with lower levels of productivity by paying lower wages. Evidence that higher skills do lead to increased firm profitability is weaker. Some research suggests that the productivity increases from higher skill levels (increased training) is twice the wage increase paid to those employees - suggesting the remaining productivity increase goes directly into firm profits (Barron, Black and Loewenstein, 1989; Blakemore and Hoffman, 1988).

**The benefits to the economy**

**2.46** The benefits of education and training may not be restricted to individuals or employers, but could spill over to the economy as a whole (the social return). At the most basic level there are obvious benefits to society from having an educated and literate population, including increased participation in democratic institutions and social cohesion.

**2.47** Our focus is mainly on the economic benefits of skills in terms of higher productivity, wages and employability. However, there is clear evidence that better educated people tend to be healthier and live longer. Education appears to lessen the risk of crime through helping to socialise young people who remain in school. Higher levels of education are also inversely related to other social outcomes which are indicators of social deprivation such as teenage pregnancy (OECD, 1998).

**2.48** It has also been argued that educated individuals in a firm, as well as being more productive themselves, can raise the productivity of their less educated colleagues (Gemmell, 1996; Redding, 1996). In a similar vein, educated parents can teach their own children. These sorts of ideas form the basis of new growth theories where the accumulation of skills and knowledge can, through such spill-over effects, lead to increasing rates of economic growth (Romer 1986). This idea that education and training provide returns to society, as well as individuals, is one of the key justifications for publicly-funded education.

**2.49** There are problems in separating out the various contributions to economic growth (e.g. the quantity of physical capital, quantity of labour, quality of labour and the technological capacity of the economy) and studies in this area frequently encounter measurement problems. Overall, the evidence indicates that both human capital and technical know-how are vitally important to economic growth. However, the evidence suggests that the effect is not homogeneous and that much more work is needed to disentangle the different effects. (Sianesi & Van Reenen, forthcoming).

**2.50** Several studies have investigated the main factors contributing to cross-country differences in economic growth rates and have found that a high average level of attainment is related to economic growth (Krueger and Lindhal, 1998). Some studies highlight the importance of attainment at the secondary level of education as an important pre-condition for rapid growth (Barro, 1991; Levine and Renelt, 1992; Barro 1997; Hanushek and Kim, 1995). Others have highlighted the importance of higher education (Gemmel, 1996) with recent evidence suggesting that a ten percent increase in the proportion of the labour force in higher education would raise GDP per person by about 3.3% (Sianesi & Van Reenen, forthcoming).

**2.51** Other researchers have sought to decompose output growth in individual countries such as the US into the respective contributions of different factors of production such as physical capital (e.g. machinery and buildings) and labour. These 'growth accounting' studies have found that a large proportion of US growth in recent decades can be 'explained' through adjustments for improvements in workforce quality as proxied by investments in education (Jorgenson, Fraumeni and Gollop, 1987). More recent evidence from the UK covering the period 1971 to 1992 suggests that a one percentage point increase in the proportion of workers with higher qualifications raises annual output by between 0.42 and 0.63% (Jenkins, 1995). These results are extremely sensitive to the measure of educational quality that is used and do not deal with the possible endogeneity of schooling (i.e. higher schooling may result from higher growth rather than the other way round).

**2.52** Many economists have suggested that educated and/or skilled labour may play a key role in determining the capacity of nations, not just to generate economically-useful knowledge, but also to identify and make good use of innovations and knowledge created elsewhere in the world (Cameron, Proudman and Redding, 1998; Griffith, Redding and Van Reenen, 1999). Benhabib and Spiegel (1994) present a theoretical model which allows for investments in human capital (investments in workforce education and training) to contribute to productivity and growth via their impact on knowledge search and utilisation. Their empirical results suggest that human capital stocks are positively associated with individual countries' ability to narrow the gap between themselves and the world-leading nation in terms of productivity. Higher levels of human capital are also found to contribute indirectly to growth by encouraging investments in physical capital.

## Summary

**2.53** In this chapter we have set out our definition of skills. They are hierarchically determined by degrees of autonomy and complexity with different dimensions (cognitive, manual) with most jobs requiring the exercise of more than one skill in more than one dimension. There are different types of skills, those that can be used across large numbers of different occupations being termed generic skills. Occupational or technical skills found predominantly within an occupation or occupational group are defined as vocational skills. Some vocational skills are transferable across occupations. Finally we have defined personal attributes as those skills that relate to personal characteristics such as motivation, judgement and leadership.

**2.54** Skills are acquired in a range of different ways. Full-time education's role is predominantly that of providing a core level of basic, generic and some practical and technical skills - the latter, particularly post-16. The work-based route plays an essential role in providing and maintaining practical and technical skills. A significant element of this practical skills formation is best suited to learning in the workplace, either through on-the-job learning or more informal methods of learning that can be practiced and reinforced in a work environment. Work experience within a full-time education context also has a role to play in developing these skills.

**2.55** Work-based learning also plays an important role in developing more generic skills and some personal attributes. Generic skills such as team working and business awareness, and attributes such as leadership and judgement are linked to maturity and experience. In this respect work-based learning will always play an essential role in bringing individuals up to their full potential.

**2.56** Skills make a significant contribution to economic success. They are needed not just to achieve the competitiveness agenda or the social exclusion agenda - they are needed for both. Skills are negatively related to indicators of social deprivation such as crime and teenage pregnancy and are positively related to better economic outcomes. Individuals have a much higher chance of becoming socially excluded if they don't work and have a much higher chance of not working if they have low levels of skill. A high level of skill can lead to a much better chance of a good income.

**2.57** Firms are more likely to have high levels of productivity if they have a skilled workforce. This is not simply the product of the number of higher skilled people they employ but the knock-on effect such individuals have on other workers and the work practices employers are able to adopt. While it has been more difficult to demonstrate, the evidence suggests that economies with a preponderance of higher skilled people enjoy higher levels of productivity which leads to greater competitiveness and stronger economic growth.

**2.58** This is the theoretical position; higher levels of skill benefit the individual, the firm and the economy. We are most concerned with the actual level of skill present in the labour market, the way those skills are deployed and the relative skill demand. This is the focus of the remainder of this report.

## REFERENCES

Barrett, A. and O'Connell, P. (1998), Does training generally work? The returns to in-company training, Discussion Paper No. 1879, London: Centre for Economic Policy Research (CEPR).

Barro, R. (1991), Economic growth in a cross-section of countries, *Quarterly Journal of Economics*, 106: 407-443.

Barro, R. (1997), Determinants of Economic Growth: A Cross-Country Empirical Study, Cambridge, MA: MIT Press.

Barron, J. M., Black, D. A., and Loewenstein, M. A. (1989), Job Matching and On-the-Job Training, *Journal of Labour Economics, 7, 1: 1-19*.

Bartel, A. (1994), Productivity Gains from the Implementation of Employee Training Programs, *Industrial Relations*. 33, 4, 411-425.

Benhabib, J. and Spiegel, M. (1994), The role of human capital in economic development: evidence from aggregate cross-country data, *Journal of Monetary Economics,* 34: 143-173.

Bishop, J. (1994). The impact of previous training on productivity and wages, in L. Lynch (ed.), *Training and the Private Sector: International Comparisons,* Chicago: University of Chicago Press.

Bishop, J. (1997). What we know about employer-provided training: a review of the literature. *Research in Labor Economics,* 17: 19-87.

Black, S. and Lynch, L. (1996). Human Capital Investments and Labor Productivity. *American Economic Review,* 86 (2): 263-7.

Blakemore, A and Hoffman, D. (1988), *Seniority Rules and productivity: An Empirical test,* mimeo, Arizona State University, Temple, September.

Blundell, R., Dearden, L. and Meghir, C. (1996), *The Determinant of Work-Related Training in Britain,* London: Institute for Fiscal Studies.

Cameron, Proudman and Redding (1998), "Productivity Convergence and International Openness", in J. Proudman, and S. Redding (eds), *Openness and Growth,* Bank of England, London.

Crafts, N and O'Mahony, M (1999) Britain's Productivity Performance. *New Economy,* 1 (1): 3-16.

Daly, A. Hitchens, D. and Wagner, K. (1985), Productivity, machinery and skills in a sample of British and German manufacturing plants, *National Institute Economic Review,* 111: 48-62.

Dearden, L. (1999), "Qualifications and earnings in Britain: How reliable are conventional estimates of the returns to education?" *IFS WP No. W99/7.*

Dearden, L. (1998), Ability, Families, Education and Earnings in Britain, *Institute for Fiscal Studies, Working Paper no.* W98/14.

Dearden, R. (1994) 'Education and Training', *Westminster Studies in Education* No. 7.

Dearden, L. Reed, H. and Van Reenen, J (1999), "Training and Corporate Productivity: *Evidence from British Panel Data"* IFS mimeo.

Gemmel, N. (1996). "Evaluating the impact of human capital stocks and accumulation on economic growth: some new evidence", *Oxford Bulletin of Economics and Statistics,* 58, 9-28.

Green, A. (1998), Core skills, key skills and general culture: in search of the common foundation in vocational education, *Education and Research in Education,* 12(1) 23-43.

Griffith, R., Redding, S., and Van Reenen, J. (1999) *"Mapping the Two Faces of R&D: Productivity, R&D, skills and trade in an OECD panel of industries"* IFS mimeo.

Hanushek, E.A. and Kim, D. (1995), "Schooling, Labor Force Quality and Economic Growth", National Bureau of Economic Research Working Paper: 5399.

Harmon, C. and Walker, I. (1995), Estimates of the Economic Return to Schooling in the UK, *American Economic Review,* 85: 1278-86.

Haskel, J. and Martin, C. (1993), Do skill shortages reduce productivity? Theory and evidence from the UK, *Economic Journal* 103: 386-394.

Ichniowski, C., K. Shaw, and G. Prennushi (1997). The effects of human resource management practices on productivity: a study of steel finishing lines. *American Economic Review,* 87, 3, 291-314.

Jenkins, H (1995), "Education and Production in the United Kingdom", Nuffield college, Oxford, Economics Discussion Paper No. 101.

Jorgenson, D.W., Gollop, F. and Fraumeni, B. (1987), *Productivity and US Economic Growth,* Cambridge, MA: Harvard University Press.

Keep, E and Mayhew, K (1999), The Assessment: Knowledge, Skills and Competitiveness, *Oxford Review of Economic Policy,* 15:1, Spring, 1-15.

Krueger, A.B. and Lindhal, M. (1998), "Education for Growth: Why and For Whom?", mimeo, Princeton University.

Levine, R and Renelt, D. (1992), "A Sensitivity Analysis of Cross-County Growth Regressions", *American Economic Review,* 82, 4, 942-963.

Lloyd-Ellis (1999), "Endogenous Technological Change and Wage Inequality." *The American Economic Review* 89:1.

Mason, G., and Finegold, D (1997), "Productivity, machinery and skills in the United States and Western Europe, *National Institute Economic Review,* 162:85-98.

Mason, G., and van Ark, B (1994), Vocational Training and Productivity Performance: An Anglo-Dutch Comparison, in McNabb, R. and Whitfield, K. (eds.), *The Market for Training,* Aldershot: Averbury.

Mason, G., van Ark, B. and Wagner, K. (1994), 'Productivity, product quality and workforce skills: food processing in four European countries', *National Institute Economic Review,* 147: 62-83.

Nickell, S. and Nicolitsas, D. (1999), Human capital, investment and innovation: what are the connections?, in R. Barrell, G. Mason, M. O'Mahony (eds.), *Productivity, Innovation and Economic Performance,* Cambridge: Cambridge University Press (forthcoming).

OECD (1994), The OECD Jobs Study, Evidence and Explanations, Part II, Paris.

OECD (1998), Human Capital Investment - An International Comparison, Paris.

O'Mahony, M. (1999) *Britain's Productivity Performance, 1950-1996: An International Perspective,* The National Institute of Economic and Social Research, London.

Prais, S. J., Jarvis, V. and Wagner, K. (1989), "Productivity and Vocational Skills in Services in Britain and Germany: Hotels *National Institute Economic Review.*

Romer, P.M. (1986) "Increasing Returns and Long-Run Growth". Journal of Political Economy, 94, 1002-1037.

Schultz, T. (1975), The value of the ability to deal with disequilibria, *Journal of Economic Literature,* 31: 199-225.

Sianesi, B. and Van Reenen, (forthcoming), The Returns to Education: A Review of the Macro-Economic Literature.

Spence, M (1973) - Job market signalling, *Quarterly Journal of Economics,* 87: 355-374.

Steedman, H. and Wagner, K. (1989), "Productivity, Machinery and Skills: Clothing Manufacturing in Britain and Germany", *National Institute Economic Review.*

Steedman, H. and Wagner, K. (1987), "A Second Look at Productivity, Machinery and Skills in Britain and Germany", *National Institute Economic Review.*

# CHAPTER 3
## CHANGES IN THE NATURE OF JOBS AND SKILL REQUIREMENTS

## Introduction

**3.1**   Any assessment of whether skill needs are being met must begin with an analysis of what skill needs are.  The weight of evidence suggests that there has been an overall increase in the average level of skill needed to do the average job in the UK.  However, within this it should be recognised that the overall job mix in society is changing, and that there are a range of jobs that demand very high and growing levels of skills, while there are others that demand a more limited and even declining range and/or level of skills.

**3.2**   In this chapter we review the evidence of which jobs now demand higher skills and/or a wider range of skills and which jobs demand fewer or a narrowing range of skills.  The rise in white-collar employment at the expense of blue-collar jobs is highlighted; a trend that is key to explaining the general upward drift in skill levels.  An important element of this is the growing professionalisation of the workforce with the related shift within intermediate level jobs from craft to associate professional employment.  We look at skills changes within occupations to assess trends in the overall demand for different types of skill.  The chapter also acknowledges that not all employment trends are towards higher level skills, with significant employment remaining in lower skilled jobs.  Few of these jobs, however, will be available for those with no skills.

**3.3**   The analysis is partly based on trends in occupations as a proxy for skills.  We highlight the drawbacks of this approach but also point to its strengths.  This occupation-based analysis is supplemented with more subjective evidence on employees' views of how skills are changing in jobs (again reflecting on the strengths and weakness of this approach).  The important skill areas where demand seems to be greatest are highlighted.  As one would expect, generic skills appear high on the list.  The analysis aims to go beyond the common approach of saying that all generic skills are important to identify those which seem to be most important.  Communication skills and problem solving skills together with the ability to organise oneself and others within a team seem to be key.

# Empirical evidence on the nature of change in jobs and skills

**3.4** One common way of investigating how skills have changed over time is to look at the changing distribution of jobs by occupation. The analysis of occupations in this chapter is based on the new classification of occupations (SOC2000). Despite the improvements in this new classification, occupations as defined in the Standard Occupational Classification (SOC) are still imperfect proxies for skills. However, data on trends in employment by SOC are more extensive than any data that purport to directly measure skill and the hierarchical nature of SOC data does give some useful pointers to how skill levels have changed. Furthermore, research based on cohort studies such as the National Child Development Study (NCDS) and the British Cohort Study (BCS), both of which have more direct measures of skills, has shown a clear relationship between skill levels and occupation: the more highly ranked the occupation, the greater the variety of skills or personal attributes reported (Bynner, 1994).

## Shift from manual to non-manual jobs

**3.5** The most striking occupation change over the past 20 years has been the shift in employment from blue-collar (manual) jobs to white collar (non-manual) jobs. As Table 3.1 shows, in 1971 51% of all jobs were to be found in SOC categories 5-6 and 8-9 covering, mainly, manual occupations. By 1998 the proportion of employment accounted for by these jobs had fallen to 43%. The decline in manual jobs has slowed in recent years and the fall in the proportion of employment accounted for by manual jobs is expected to be more modest over the period to 2009.

**3.6** The expansion in white-collar work has seen the creation of millions of jobs in the managerial, professional and associate professional categories (increasing from 27% to 36% of the workforce between 1971 and 1998). These types of jobs demand high levels of technical, cognitive and problem-solving skills. Research on senior managers has stressed the need for organisational, conceptual and people management skills (Kettley and Strebler, 1997). It is not surprising therefore that, given these changes in the occupational structure of the labour force, we have seen greater demands for these types of skills.

**3.7** This growth in non-manual jobs and the demand for related skills is partly attributable to the industrial shifts that have affected the economy. As Table 3.2 illustrates, in 1971 manufacturing accounted for 32% of employment. Within this sector manual jobs made up around 63% of employment. Employment in the market and non-market service sector accounted for 30% of employment but here the majority (nearly 70%) of jobs were non-manual. The growth in employment in the service industries (accounting for 47% of employment in 1998) and decline in manufacturing (accounting for 16% of employment in 1998) directly explain a significant amount of the shift towards non-manual employment in this period.

**Table 3.1: Employment trends by occupation 1971-1998 and projections for 2009, UK**

| | | 1971 | 1981 | 1991 | 1998 | 2009 |
|---|---|---|---|---|---|---|
| | **Total Employment (millions)** | **24.4** | **24.5** | **26.0** | **27.1** | **29.4** |
| | | Percent of total employment | | | | |
| 1 | Managers and Senior Officials | 11 | 10 | 13 | 13 | 13 |
| 2 | Professional Occupations | 7 | 8 | 9 | 11 | 13 |
| 3 | Associate Professional and Technical Occupations | 9 | 9 | 11 | 12 | 14 |
| 4 | Administrative, Clerical & Secretarial Occupations | 14 | 16 | 16 | 15 | 14 |
| 5 | Skilled Trade Occupations | 19 | 17 | 15 | 14 | 12 |
| 6 | Personal Service Occupations | 3 | 4 | 5 | 6 | 7 |
| 7 | Sales & Customer Service Occupations | 5 | 6 | 6 | 7 | 7 |
| 8 | Process, Plant & Machine Operatives | 14 | 12 | 10 | 9 | 8 |
| 9 | Elementary Occupations | 17 | 18 | 15 | 14 | 12 |
| | **All Occupations** | **100** | **100** | **100** | **100** | **100** |

Source: Wilson, (2000)

**Table 3.2: Employment by industry 1971-1998 and projections for 2004 and 2009, UK**

| | 1971 | 1981 | 1991 | 1998 | 2009 |
|---|---|---|---|---|---|
| **Total Employment (millions)** | **24.4** | **24.5** | **26.0** | **27.1** | **29.4** |
| | Percent of total employment | | | | |
| Primary and Utilities | 7 | 6 | 4 | 3 | 2 |
| Manufacturing | 32 | 25 | 18 | 16 | 13 |
| Construction | 7 | 6 | 7 | 7 | 6 |
| Distribution, Transport etc. | 26 | 27 | 28 | 28 | 28 |
| Business & Miscellaneous Services | 12 | 15 | 20 | 24 | 29 |
| Non-market Services | 18 | 21 | 23 | 23 | 22 |
| **All Industries** | **100** | **100** | **100** | **100** | **100** |

Source: Wilson (2000)

**3.8** However, the shift towards non-manual jobs and skills is not completely explained by the industrial shift in employment. There has also been a significant movement towards white-collar jobs in sectors which have traditionally employed a large proportion of blue-collar workers. The proportion of non-production workers in the manufacturing sector has increased from 35% in 1971 to 43% in 1998 despite the significant outsourcing of many functions during the last decade. This growth has been particularly noticeable among managerial occupations. In 1971 7% of the manufacturing workforce was accounted for by managerial jobs; by 1998 this had increased to 12%.

**3.9** In more recent years the impact of organisational and technological changes on the occupational structure of employment within industries has probably had a more marked effect on overall occupational change than shifts in industrial composition. Once overall scale effects (i.e. overall growth in jobs) are accounted for, about 55% of the growth in non-manual jobs between 1990 and 1998 can be attributed to changes within industries with the remainder being accounted for by changes in industrial composition. For non-manual jobs a similar pattern emerges with 55% of the gross decline (i.e. not taking into account scale effects) in non-manual jobs being due to the impact of organisational and technological change within industries with the remainder being due to manual jobs being more likely to be in industries experiencing job losses (Wilson, 2000).

**3.10** Not all non-manual job growth has been in higher skilled areas. There has been significant growth in lower skilled occupations such as certain personal service occupations (containing jobs such as security guards, nursery nurses and hairdressers) and more modest growth in sales and customer service occupations. However, while these occupations require relatively low levels of prior training, they do place great emphasis on specific types of skill, particularly inter-personal skills and communication skills. We return to the growing demand for these types of skill later in the report.

## Changing composition of intermediate level jobs

**3.11** Intermediate level jobs range from associate professional occupations through to clerical and secretarial occupations and craft and skilled manual jobs. Overall employment in intermediate level jobs has increased modestly from 10.4m jobs in 1981 to 11.1m in 1998 with a projected growth to 11.7m in 2009.

**3.12** The significant trend within intermediate level jobs is the shift from employment in blue-collar jobs (e.g. skilled trade jobs) towards employment in white-collar ones (associate professional and technical occupations). In 1971 there were over twice as many skilled trade jobs as there were associate professional ones. By 1998 the numbers employed in associate professional jobs were roughly the same as in skilled trade jobs and by 2009 we expect associate professionals to outnumber skilled trade workers by 17%.

**3.13** This shift in the composition of intermediate level employment is largely explained by three factors:

- falling overall employment in <u>manufacturing, primary and utilities,</u> particularly during the 1980s, which traditionally have had a high proportion of skilled trade jobs especially in metal and electrical trades

- falling employment in metal and electrical trade and construction occupations <u>throughout the economy</u> during the 1990s as new technology has reduced the demand for these types of workers

- increased employment in associate professional occupations in business services (e.g. accountants, finance analysts) and design and leisure-related activities (such as culture and sport)

An increasing proportion of intermediate level jobs in the labour market are found in financial, media, design, sales and marketing occupations. In these areas skill needs centre on creativity and associated technical abilities plus an awareness of business performance and its place in the market.

**3.14** While skilled trade employment has fallen in manufacturing, this does not necessarily mean that skilled trade skills have become less important in the production process. In manufacturing in 1971 there were 12 skilled trade jobs (excluding those employed in agricultural trades) for every technician (science associate professional) job. In 1998 the ratio of skilled trade to technician level jobs in manufacturing was slightly less at 10:1. The ratio of skilled trade jobs to operator and elementary production workers (unskilled) has increased slightly between 1971 and 1998 in manufacturing (from 1 skilled trade job to every operator/elementary job to 1.14 skilled trade to every operator/ elementary job). There are now more skilled trade jobs than unskilled production jobs in manufacturing.[1]

**3.15** Furthermore, while overall numbers of skilled trade jobs have declined, and will continue to do so, there will continue to be significant numbers of job opportunities at this level. This is because the age profile of many skilled trade occupations is relatively old (for example, 38% of workers in metal machining and fitting trades are aged over 45 compared to 31% of the total labour force) and future retirement rates will exceed job losses resulting in substantial net demand for craft level workers. Forecasts suggest that, despite an overall decline of 265,000 in skilled trade jobs to 2009, there will be a need for nearly 1.3 million new people in these jobs to meet replacement demand.

**3.16** Skilled trade jobs also remain important because of the changing nature of these types of jobs. Fewer of these jobs are solely concerned with production functions. More skilled trade workers are expected to be multi-functional. They are expected to take responsibility for a wider range of tasks related to a particular product including: scheduling, ordering, managing customer relations, programming (Computer Numerically Controlled machinery) and maintenance. This has resulted in a greater blurring of the boundary between traditional craft and technician level jobs and a widening in the skills needed by many craft level workers (Finegold and Wagner, 1999).

---

[1] Technician is taken as SOC code 3, craft as 52 and 54, and operative and elementary production worker as 81.

## Growth in professional jobs

**3.17** The number of jobs in professional occupations increased by 50% between 1981 and 1998. Professional jobs are expected to be one of the fastest growing occupations through to 2009 with a further expansion of over 20% or nearly 867,000 jobs forecast. Employment in these areas requires a varied range of skills from those needed to be doctors to those needed to be accountants. However, invariably they are specialist skills requiring a higher education. There is also a growing demand for people in these jobs to have good communication skills to find out what their customers want and explain technical issues to their client base.

**3.18** Much of the growth in employment in professional jobs, can be explained by the expansion of the service sectors (both private and public). Indeed employment of professionals has become even more concentrated in these two sectors of the labour market since 1971. In that year 68% of professional and associate professional jobs were to be found in the public and private service sectors compared with 80% in 1998.

**3.19** However, while the numbers of professionals employed outside the service industries overall have not increased significantly, their importance in areas such as manufacturing has risen greatly. The largest group of professionals employed in manufacturing are science and technical professionals. The numbers employed in this category have remained static at around 18,000 since 1971 but, as a proportion of total employment in manufacturing, they now make up nearly 4% of the workforce compared to just over 2% in 1971. Professional and technical staff have been key in delivering the technological improvements that have enabled the productivity gains achieved in manufacturing in recent years. It is these technological changes that have enabled the numbers of workers at other levels to be reduced (with the exception of managers involved in delivering accompanying changes in work organisation).

## Employment remains significant in low-skill jobs

**3.20** There is still a significant element of employment in relatively low-skilled jobs. The total numbers employed in personal service, sales and customer service, operative and elementary occupations fell only slightly between 1981 and 1998 (by 200,000 jobs). Forecasts suggest that the numbers of jobs in these categories will actually rise through to 2009. However, growth is likely to be confined to semi-skilled personal service and sales occupations while the numbers employed in the predominantly unskilled operative and elementary occupations will continue to fall.

**3.21** On the other hand, job turnover in unskilled and semi-skilled occupations is relatively high and together with the need to replace retirements this will create large numbers of new job opportunities in these areas. Between now and 2009 we expect there to be over $2^1/_2$ million job opportunities in semi-skilled personal service and sales occupations and nearly $2^3/_4$ million job opportunities in unskilled operative and elementary occupations.

**3.22** But most importantly, in terms of skills, while personal service and sales jobs call for relatively low levels of skill, the nature of the skills they do require is changing. Few of the jobs will call for no skills at all. Many of these jobs will be in areas where there is an increased premium on communication and customer care skills. We turn to the changing demand for skills within occupations in the next section.

## Overall increase in skill needs

3.23   Changes in the occupational structure conceal changes in skills within occupational groups. Despite this, there is relatively little research which looks directly at the range of skills and their distribution in the labour force.  In the US, one approach to this type of research has been to use the US Department of Commerce's Dictionary of Occupational Titles (DOT).  DOT is based on inspectors observing employee skill levels in the workplace.  There is also a large body of research in the US based on employers' or managers' perceptions of skills change.

3.24  In the UK, research has focused on employee perceptions of skill change in studies such as the Social Change and Economic Life Initiative (SCELI) (Gallie, 1991), the Employment in Britain Survey (Gallie and White 1993) and the Skills Survey (Ashton et al 1999).  The research can be criticised on the basis that it relies in part on individual perceptions of the skills they need and use, and that it relies on recall when considering change over time.  However, the results from the research show a clear relationship between reported skill levels and the skill levels one would expect within the occupational hierarchy, for example, managers and professionals report much higher skill levels than semi-skilled and unskilled workers.  The research also demonstrates a clear positive relationship between earnings and reported skill levels as one would expect.  This suggests that the skill measures used in the research are corroborated by other evidence.

3.25  In each of the three surveys (SCELI, Employment in Britain and the Skills Survey) it was reported that a substantial balance of respondents perceived that their skills were rising.  Comparing the surveys, it was found that over time increasing numbers of people were in jobs that required long training times.  Moreover, increasing numbers were in jobs that would take at least six months actually doing that type of work before the jobs could be done well.  Long learning time is seen as a sign of job complexity.  In addition, reported qualification levels needed to get jobs have also been increasing over time, according to these surveys.

3.26  Some researchers have argued that the rise in demand for qualifications by employers reflects increased credentialism and that there has been a qualifications inflation rather than a substantial upskilling of jobs (Robinson and Manacorda, 1997; Giret and Masjun, 1999; Espinasse and Vincens, 1997).  However, this argument tends to ignore the pervasive nature of technological change, in IT in particular, that is driving skills growth across many sectors of the economy.  The evidence on this issue from the job content analysis studies referred to above suggests that the higher qualifications demanded by employers are widely viewed by employees as necessary to do the jobs in question.  If employers had needlessly raised their desired qualification levels, we would have expected these surveys to show significantly more employees saying in 1997 that their qualifications were not needed for actually doing the job.  This was not the case (Ashton et al, 1999).

**3.27** Further work by Wilson using the survey data found that skill demands were likely to continue to rise in the future (Wilson 2000). However, findings from SCELI (Gallie, 1991) and the Employment in Britain Survey (Gallie and White, 1993) suggested that skill increases are not uniform across the labour market. Low-skilled manual workers were much less likely to have experienced an increase in skill levels than their counterparts in intermediate and higher level occupations. Women were found to report much lower levels of skill increases than men. The research concluded that this was due to these groups having much less exposure to advanced technologies and, particularly in the case of women, to their higher levels of part-time working. Higher skill levels among intermediate and higher level occupations were found to be related to increased task discretion in these jobs, their widespread use of computer technology and increases in levels of job responsibility.

**3.28** The more recent Skills Survey shows those in managerial, professional and associate professional jobs were around 50% more likely to have reported an increase in skill levels than those in sales, operative or general labouring jobs (Table 3.3). However, other indicators paint a more complex picture with some skill needs rising faster for lower level jobs.

**Table 3.3: Employee perceptions of skill change**

| Selected characteristics | Perceptions of skills change | |
|---|---|---|
| | Percentage increase | Percentage decrease |
| **By occupation in 1997** | | |
| Managers | 68.4 | 6.6 |
| Professionals | 62.7 | 1.7 |
| Associate professionals | 71.7 | 6.4 |
| Clerical & secretarial | 69.2 | 10.7 |
| Craft & related | 51.8 | 6.9 |
| Personal & protective services | 56.4 | 11.4 |
| Sales | 46.5 | 17.1 |
| Plant & machine operatives | 46.6 | 13.1 |
| Other | 41.6 | 12.8 |

Source: Felstead et al (2000)

**3.29** All the generic skills, including IT skills, were more evenly spread across the population in 1997 than they had been five years previously (Felstead et al, 2000). Moreover, broad measures of work skills show women's job skills catching up on men's job skills between 1986 and 1997. However, the skills involved in jobs for part-time women are on average much lower than for the rest of the population and continue to lag behind. Women who switch from full to part-time employment often take jobs requiring lower skills (Green et al 2000). There is evidence that part-time women's skills and educational qualifications are more likely to be under-utilised than those of any other group in the population (Bynner, 1994; Bynner et al, 1996).

**3.30** Most occupations reported experiencing an increase in skills. In 1997 it was only in the case of general labouring jobs ("other occupations") that the proportion saying there had been no change in skill levels was greater than those saying that there had been an increase. However, there are pockets of the labour market where skill levels are not increasing very much. It is clear that skill levels in most clerical, operative and personal service occupations remain considerably lower than in intermediate and professional jobs.

## Why are skill needs changing?

**3.31** As is well known, there are several competing explanations for the increased relative demand for skilled employees and the resulting growth in inequality of wages and salaries that has occurred. Many researchers argue that the key factor driving the changes is the bias against low-skilled workers associated with the introduction of new technologies (Katz and Murphy, 1992; Allen, 1996; Machin, 1996; Berman, Bound and Machin, 1998). Others emphasise changes in trade patterns and the growing import competition from low-wage countries which have obliged many producers in high wage nations to move into higher value added, more skill-intensive product areas (Wood, 1995). It is likely that a full explanation of rising skill requirements in advanced industrial nations would give some weight to all these factors since competition from low-cost imports is often a stimulus for the introduction of new technology and more efficient work practices.

### Changing skill needs and new technology

**3.32** There is a well established and on-going debate over whether technological change predominantly results in a de-skilling of the workforce (mainly through the automation of production processes) or upskilling (mainly through the broadening of jobs and the upgrading of skill needs). In many ways, this is a sterile debate. The issue is not which theory is right but which processes dominate. The weight of evidence suggests that the predominant impact of technological change in recent years has been to demand, certainly, a wider range and, probably, a higher level of skill from the workforce.

**3.33** This is because technologies are much more integrated in the modern economy, and today's worker needs to better understand the role of individual machines and pieces of equipment in the continuous work process. In the manufacturing sector, this has manifested itself in a shift in skill requirements from dexterity and other manual competences towards cognitive abilities, and from skills related to a particular material or substance to skills related to machinery and production processes. "...On the one hand this means that 'system skills', including organisational and technical knowledge and abilities, are required; on the other hand, workers have to be able to work in teams, with an emphasis on behavioural skills..." (Thompson et al, 1995).

**3.34** There is a much greater emphasis on skills related to monitoring and troubleshooting to keep the work process flowing. Steedman (1999) notes that in the water industry the introduction of more advanced control technologies mean that;

*"operators no longer observe or taste the water flowing through the plant but interpret information in alpha numerical format relayed from numerical test equipment...Instead of interpreting physical phenomena using primary senses, [operators] work from the abstract representation of the phenomena.. the operator must act immediately to unpredictable physical changes monitored and represented in abstract form and take appropriate remedial action"*

**3.35** New technology has resulted in a higher demand for maintenance skills for automated equipment and a move from the manual guiding of machinery to its monitoring by sight and sound. Rather than working one machine, workers today oversee several machines; machines that are much more complex and with tighter tolerances than ever before. For example, the introduction of Computer Numerically Controlled (CNC) machine tools has greatly reduced the need for craft workers to physically handle tools, with a resulting reduction in demand for related skills, but this has led to new skills demands to programme machines and for workers to run a number of machines simultaneously. Rather than being able to feel whether a machine tool was about to make an inappropriate cut, workers now needed be able to hear whether the machine is working the metal properly (Attewell 1992, Senker 1992).

**3.36** The largest and most pervasive technological change that has impacted on skills in recent years has been the introduction of information, communication and control technologies. Caselli (1999) suggests that the development of Information Technology has constituted a skill-biased 'revolution' which has increased demand for 'low learning cost' individuals who require relatively little time to learn how to make productive use of new microelectronics-based technologies. Such learning ability is typically associated with high levels of cognitive skills rather than manual skills.

**3.37** Much of the evidence relating to recent changes in skill and/or wage structures to computer usage is based on US experience (Krueger, 1993; Autor, Katz and Krueger, 1998). However, a similarly strong association between the diffusion of Information Technology and increased relative demand for certain types of skill has now been established for the UK. Firstly, Haskel and Heden (1999) have shown that computerisation is significantly correlated with increased demand for skilled non-manual workers in UK manufacturing establishments and with lower demand for both skilled and unskilled manual workers. This latter finding highlights the reduced importance of manual skills in the new technological environment. Secondly, Green et al (1999) show that computer usage in the UK is strongly associated with a composite measure of skill intensity based on the qualification levels and training times required for different types of job together with the estimated length of time needed to achieve competence in those jobs.

**3.38** In a related study, Green (1999) is able to distinguish between different types of use of computers on a four-point scale (ranging from 'straightforward' through 'moderate' and 'complex' to 'advanced') and presents estimates of positive salary premia associated with computer use rising from 13% in the case of moderate male users (for example, those using computers for word processing, spread sheeting and/or email communications) to 21% for advanced male users (for example, those undertaking computer programming activities). For female computer users the equivalent salary premia are, respectively, 13% and 15%. These results are based on a nationally representative survey of individuals in paid employment in 1997 and control for individuals' work experience, education levels and diverse job characteristics.

**3.39** This is not to say that the introduction of new technology automatically results in demands for higher levels or a wider range of skills. There are many instances where new technology has resulted in a lower demand for skills and narrower job descriptions by, for example, 'automating out' the demand for many craft skills (Lloyd, 1997, Rolfe 1986). The actual impact new technology has on skill levels will be determined by the way the new technology is introduced and, in particular, the work organisation prevalent in the firm. Senker (1992) argues that the conservative approach by many UK managers and the inflexibility inherent in the single skill craft system have acted as a barrier to the full exploitation of new technology in the UK.

## Skill needs and changing work organisation

**3.40** A second debate that has raged on the factors driving skill change has focused on the extent to which firms are competing on price or on quality. Researchers who see firms as competing on price are more inclined to see a lower level of skill demand in the economy as firms competing in such markets are seen to produce large quantities of low value-added products requiring little skilled input (Keep and Mayhew, 1998). Commentators who see firms as competing on quality emphasise the other end of the spectrum. They are more inclined to see higher skill demands as firms competing on quality are seen to produce short-run, custom-made products where the ability to rapidly change the production process and achieve high levels of quality are dependent on high levels of skills (Attewell, 1992).

**3.41** These two positions are set out to emphasise the extremes. Many firms would argue that they compete on price while simultaneously producing a high quality product. The ways they have attempted to achieve this is to organise work such that quality procedures are an integral part of the work process (for example by using Total Quality Management (TQM) or Quality Circles) and production is as efficient as possible by reducing stock (Just-in-Time methods) and making the most effective use of labour (multi-skilling and multi-functioning). Recent research by Finegold and Wagner suggests that these "lean production" methods are a key way in which firms can reduce costs while maintaining or improving the quality and range of products. (Finegold and Wagner, 1999)

**3.42** "Lean production" is best achieved where work is organised in a flexible manner; where a full range of skills are available to an integrated work process. The extent to which this has been achieved in the UK has been uneven as we discuss later in this chapter in the context of a growing need for management skills. However, there is evidence that changes in work practices in the UK, related to the drive for higher quality and lower costs, have led to a greater emphasis on team working as a means of effectively pooling skills and organising work. The 1998 Workplace Employers Relations Survey found that 83% of managers stated that at least some employees in their largest occupational group worked in formal designated teams, and in 65% of workplaces most employees in the group worked in teams (Cully, 1999).

**3.43** In many industries, such as engineering, the growth in cell-working and team-working has led to higher levels of task discretion and individual responsibility from all categories of employee except for the very lowest-skilled (Mason, 1999a). The spread of 'high-involvement' work practices such as team-working also helps to explain why engineering employers who identify skill gaps in their workforce put so much emphasis on deficiencies in personal, communication and problem-solving skills alongside the practical skills which are needed (EMTA, 1999).

**3.44** The apparent growth in employer demand for these generic skills has been especially striking at the graduate level, particularly for technical graduates, resulting in an apparent increase in the level of difficulty associated with 'entry jobs' for new graduates. Some 47% of recruiting enterprises in a UK survey of employers of technical graduates in 1998 said that new graduates' jobs had become 'much more complex and demanding' in recent years and another 29% replied that the jobs were 'no more complex but more pressured and demanding' (Mason, 1999b). The single most important reason cited for jobs becoming more complex and demanding was the need for graduates to take more responsibility at an earlier stage of their career - largely as a result of de-layering and the reduced scope for new graduates to receive long induction programmes, or detailed supervision in their work (ibid).

**3.45** It is important to put the speed of change in skill demands within firms and the economy at large into historical perspective. The most important technological and work practice innovations, including those with the most profound effect on industries, often take many years to diffuse completely. Moreover, such technologies and work practices are rarely if ever introduced in a once and for all manner. Typically, such innovations are introduced piecemeal and are subject to on-going modifications to the original equipment or work practices. From this perspective, skill change is often evolutionary in nature as firms who introduce new technology or work practices commit themselves to lengthy periods of experimentation and skill development. This process typically benefits from having a highly skilled and committed workforce in the first place. It places a premium on workers to be flexible, demonstrate initiative and a willingness to learn and relearn (Attewell 1992).

## Trends in demand for specific skills

**3.46** Thus far the emphasis in this chapter has been on changes in demand for skills associated with changes in occupational and industrial structure and with changes in technology, markets and work organisation. However, it is important to recognise that these overall trends often hide more complex changes in skill needs within and between occupations.

## Communication skills

3.47 In many advanced industrial countries such as Britain there is now widespread evidence of increased relative demand for certain types of skill, in particular, cognitive and interpersonal skills. As Table 3.4 shows, respondents to the Skills Survey state quite clearly that the demands for problem solving, communication and social skills have increased in the five years to 1997. We return below to the issue of the increased demand for cognitive skills. Here we focus on what types of communications skills are in demand, where and why.

**Table 3.4: Type of work skill changes in Britain 1992 - 1997 (All occupations)**

| Skill type | Percentage increasing | Percentage decreasing |
|---|---|---|
| **Problem-solving skills** | | |
| e.g. • Thinking of solutions to problems or faults | 34.1 | 19.9 |
| • Analysing complex problems in depth | 39.3 | 18.6 |
| **Communication and social skills** | | |
| e.g. • Persuading or influencing others | 36.4 | 21.8 |
| • Counselling, advising or caring for customers or clients | 36.9 | 14.6 |
| • Working with a team of people | 34.9 | 17.8 |
| **Manual skills** | | |
| e.g. • Physical stamina | 20.2 | 31.0 |
| • Skill or accuracy in using hands or fingers | 23.1 | 29.0 |
| **Computing skills** | | |
| e.g. • Using a computer, PC, or other types of computerised equipment | 42.0 | 10.4 |
| • Level of computer usage | 29.2 | 6.1 |

Source: Green et al (2000)

3.48 As we become richer many of us demand a better, larger and more sophisticated range of products and services. We expect those we come into contact with to be articulate and helpful in explaining and selling this better, larger and more sophisticated range of products and services to us. There has been a shift in culture in recent years towards "customer service" which is seen as the only way to gain competitive advantage in many sectors.

**3.49** In the business, finance and retail sectors this has led to greater employment in customer service and marketing jobs which place greatest emphasis on interpersonal skills: the ability to communicate with clients and solve problems related to client needs. The Employers' Skill Survey (ESS) found that 71% of all firms required new or additional customer handling skills, and 68% required new or additional communication skills in order to move into higher quality product or service areas. In offices, secretaries now play a much greater role throughout the organisation, serving a greater number of managers and liaising with an increasing range of staff. The ability to communicate at different levels within the hierarchy is now essential for these types of jobs (Giles, La Valle and Perryman, 1996).

**3.50** It is not just customer-orientated jobs where the demand for inter personal skills, and particularly communications skills, have risen. Indeed, the dispersal of the need for these skills throughout the economy is perhaps most marked in areas where these skills were not previously considered important, e.g. at craft level in manufacturing. Today there is a growing need for these skills on the shopfloor as workers are organised more into cells or teams and with a greater range of workers coming into contact with clients. The Skills Survey found that the largest increase in employees perceiving a growing need for instructing and advising skills was among craft workers (Green et al, 2000). However, the ESS suggested that these trends can be overstated (see Chapter 5)

## Cognitive skills and greater autonomy

**3.51** As we defined the term in Chapter 1, cognitive skills are needed among other things to be able to identify problems and find solutions. An individual is more likely to be applying these skills if he or she is working in a relatively autonomous environment where he or she has some responsibility for decision making. There has been a growing demand for these types of skills in the labour market as is shown from the proportion of respondents to the Skills Survey reporting an increased need for problem-solving skills.

**3.52** One of the greatest changes in skill levels within occupations that has resulted in rising demands for cognitive skills has been at craft and operator level in some branches of manufacturing. While new technologies have reduced the demand for manual skills in these jobs, the need to oversee and maintain equipment and work within a more complex production environment has led to a rising demand for thinking, reasoning and problem-solving skills. The environment is more complex because the shopfloor now contains a mixture of computerised and mechanised machines. Furthermore, new technology may not be more error-prone than its predecessors but the integration of different types of equipment means that the production process is more vulnerable to failure at any one point in the system. Hence, when machines go down, steps need to be taken immediately to ensure that the whole production process is not disrupted.

**3.53** Research in the US suggests that the new skills needed of shopfloor workers can be characterised by increased responsibility, care, attention and initiative (Hirschhorn, 1984; Adler, 1986a and 1986b). Workers need to take responsibility to reduce the risk of equipment failure and to diagnose in advance when it may happen and find solutions if it does. In the UK, O'Farrell and Oakey (1993) found that new skills were needed to programme and maintain the newly introduced CNC machinery and to achieve full benefits from its flexibility. In addition, craft-skilled workers were still frequently called upon to set and operate conventional machine tools while CNC equipment was working smoothly.

**3.54** The increase in cognitive skills and enhanced responsibility has not been confined to the manufacturing sector. In the hotel and catering sector, the employer case studies have shown that increased decentralisation now means there is a growing demand for chefs to have team leadership, communication, financial and other management skills (Rowley et al, 2000) Also in the telecommunications sector, a move away from 'pure' manufacturing to supply chain management and systems integration, increased software and services content is raising the need for greater business and commercial awareness and knowledge (Hendry et al, 2000).

**IT and new technology skills**

**3.55** The introduction of new technologies produces skill demands for people to build, develop, maintain and use those technologies. The spread of Information Technology offers the best example of this today. It is estimated that in 1992 approximately 25% of workers used IT in their job, by 1999 this had risen to over 60%. There are now over 18 million workers using IT equipment of some kind in their jobs compared to $11^{1}/_{2}$ million in 1992. In addition there are a further 800,000 people employed as IT specialists of one kind or another; up 300,000 from 1992 (ITNTO, 1999).

**3.56** The widespread use of IT in the workplace is a relatively recent phenomenon. Twenty years ago most workers would have had little contact with IT equipment on a day-to-day basis. With the introduction of IT, there has been a rapidly growing demand for jobholders to be aware of the potential of IT equipment and to become familiar with how different microelectronics-based machines or software packages operate. The speed of this change is illustrated by the fact that 42% of respondents to the Skills Survey said that their use of a computer, PC or other type of computerised equipment has increased in the 5 years to 1997.

**3.57** The demand for generic IT user skills has been particularly marked among managers. Around 48% of managers responding to the Skills Survey said that their use of computers had increased over the past five years. This was the highest of all occupational groups except professionals (which includes IT specialists). In manufacturing, this increased IT use by managers appears to be related to the widespread introduction of management information systems (MIS) that capture a mass of transactional and production data from the shopfloor. Managers are able to access and manipulate this data using PC-based data packages in a way they were not able to do before when they relied on verbal or written reports from the foreman or shopfloor supervisor (Attewell, 1992).

**3.58** The demand for specialist IT skills has been equally as spectacular. This has been related to the general pervasive spread of IT equipment in factories and offices plus demands from one-off projects such as the Year 2000 data change problem and European Monetary Union. Demand for these skills is expected to continue to be driven by developments such as the growing use of the Internet (and Intranets) for business-to-business communications (e-commerce) and the wider application of combined voice-data systems. Projections from the Institute of Employment Research at the University of Warwick suggest that the IT services industry alone will need to recruit over 540,000 people between 1998 and 2009 (Hasluck 2000).

**3.59** The present convergence of computing and telecommunications technologies is now providing the foundation for a new kind of 'market convergence' as many companies with their roots in different industries (such as computer hardware, software, telecommunications equipment and telecommunications services) strive to compete in the provision of high value-added, high-margin computing and communications services. Examples of such services include network design, installation, operation and maintenance, and IT systems integration and outsourcing. Employers active in these software-intensive areas report that they need people who combine up-to-date technical knowledge and problem-solving ability with good communications skills and the capacity to 'understand other people's businesses'. These high expectations relate to existing staff as much as to potential new recruits.

**3.60** The influence of other <u>new technologies</u> is less widespread than is the case for IT. Nevertheless there are still significant skill demands emerging from the development of new technologies such as advanced materials (polymers, ceramics and high performance metals), biotechnology, and opto-electronics (lasers, photonics). Many developments in these sectors are leading-edge and there are significant skill needs in the R&D area with a large demand for professional technical skills.

**3.61** A key feature of the technical skills demanded in most new technology areas is that they cut across many traditional disciplines. Skills needed in new materials are often a combination of those traditionally gained in physics, chemistry, metallurgy, ceramics, mathematics and computer science courses. The biotechnology sector needs those who understand the fundamentals of biology and engineering. Opto-electronics involves a technology fusion of optical and electronic techniques.

**3.62** Firms involved in these new technologies are not only looking for professional and technical people with these types of multi-disciplinary skills. They are also looking for those who can apply technical and theoretical knowledge in these disciplines to production technologies, fabrication and assembly, that is, to the general manufacturing process in order to meet ever-decreasing product development cycles.

**3.63** A final set of skill needs common to these new technology areas is a combination of project management skills and entrepreneurial skills. Project management is needed to manage the complex process of moving from laboratory testing to full scale manufacturing while maintaining the creative environment necessary in these new technology areas. Entrepreneurship is essentially about the inclination and ability to commercialise new scientific ideas. It is also about the ability to develop extended alliances (negotiation skills) to organise and finance the development of new technology from laboratory to manufacturing plant (Hendry, 1999).

## Management skills

**3.64** A central feature of the new work practices introduced by many organisations is to remove traditional systems of management control where decisions were taken on the basis of formal rules and bureaucratic structures. Many firms face uncertain and unpredictable demand. In this environment they can gain a competitive advantage from tracking customer demand quickly and responding rapidly to changes in that demand. This requires that firms and their workers are flexible and can achieve fast development times (Cappelli et al, 1997).

**3.65** Some organisations have increased their flexibility by pushing decision making further down the organisation. In such firms, individuals now take the day-to-day decisions previously taken by managers and teams have replaced traditional management structures. This reflects a belief that individuals directly involved in the work are better placed to react quickly and anticipate changing circumstances. These trends have often led to the removal of a tier of middle management in many large organisations and have increased autonomy and responsibility at low levels of the hierarchy.

**3.66** Efforts to match Japanese levels of quality assurance and efficiency have led to some introducing Total Quality Management (TQM), Quality Circles, Just-in-time delivery systems and other new work practices. There has been some debate over how widespread the introduction of these new practices has been and the extent to which firms have introduced the full range of new work practices. Waterson et al (1999) found that the majority of manufacturing firms say they use at least some new working practices to some extent (see Table 3.5). These techniques all place greater emphasis on teams of workers to solve shop floor quality problems which in turn reduces the need for large numbers of middle managers and supervisors (Cappelli 1997).

**Table 3.5: Extent of use of management practices in UK in 1996**

| | Percentage of sites which use the practice | | |
|---|---|---|---|
| | Not at all | A little - moderate | A lot - entirely |
| Empowerment | 28 | 49 | 23 |
| Team-based Working | 30 | 36 | 35 |
| Just-in-time Production | 29 | 31 | 40 |
| Total Quality Management | 26 | 32 | 43 |

Source: Waterson et al (1999)

**3.67** Before the 1980s, these types of management practices were not commonly utilised. Less than 10% of companies had introduced these management practices prior to 1980, while around 18% introduced these practices between 1980 and 1989. It can clearly be seen in Table 3.6 that the uptake of these practices has mainly occurred in the 1990s with an average of 75% of firms introducing the four highlighted management practices between 1990 and 1997.

**Table 3.6: Year of introduction of practices**

| | Percentage of companies that introduced practice during specified time period | | | | |
|---|---|---|---|---|---|
| | Before 1960 | 1960-1969 | 1970-1979 | 1980-1989 | 1990-1997 |
| Empowerment | 1 | 1 | 4 | 14 | 81 |
| Team-based Working | 1 | 1 | 4 | 16 | 77 |
| Just-in-time Production | 2 | 2 | 8 | 23 | 65 |
| Total Quality Management | 0 | 1 | 3 | 17 | 78 |

Source: Waterson et al (1999)

**3.68** These changes have led to an increase in the demand for traditional management type skills (e.g. work allocation, work organisation, decision-making) at lower levels. For example, the 1992 Employment in Britain Survey shows that nearly two-thirds of employees surveyed thought that the level of responsibility in their job had increased during the previous five years and that task discretion had increased during the late 1980s and early 1990s. The subsequent Skills Survey carried out in 1997 did not find a similar increase in autonomy though it did find an increase in workers reporting greater need for related management skills such as problem-solving and influencing others.

**3.69** The Skills Survey did show that, while managers are the most likely to say that they have a great deal of choice in the way they do their job, significant numbers in other occupations say they have a similar amount of discretion. Over half of those in craft level jobs, and more than 4 out of 10 people in clerical/secretarial and personal and protective service jobs, say that they had a great deal of choice in the way they do their job. Similarly, while 4 in 10 managers say they are not at all closely supervised in the work they do, over one in five workers in all other occupations responding to the Skills Survey claimed that they had similar amounts of autonomy in their working lives.

**3.70** It is possible to overstate the impact these developments are having on the demand for management-type skills among non-management and supervisory staff. The introduction of these new work practices is patchy and uneven and only in leading-edge companies would we expect all of them to be widespread. There is still a significant demand for traditional management and supervisory staff in both the manufacturing and service sectors.

**3.71** Changes in work practices have radically altered the mix of skills needed by first-line managers and supervisors. In manufacturing industries, production supervisors now need the ability to plan and communicate with customers as their responsibilities widen and they also need higher levels of technical understanding to liaise with maintenance staff (Steedman, Mason and Wagner, 1991). In addition, the recent growth in team-working has in many cases 'freed' supervisors to take a more strategic approach to improving shopfloor efficiency and to participating in cross-functional product development teams (Mason 1999c).

**3.72** Research also suggests a growing demand for more multi-skilled senior managers. Within many firms, senior managers now run separate business units for particular products and have full profit and loss responsibilities for those elements of their firms. They have broader spans of command and need to be better all-rounders imparting a strategic direction to their business units in order to cope with rapidly changing market places. The skills needed of senior managers have been defined by Kettley and Strebler (1997) as:

- Organisational skills and technical know-how required to manage operations, monitor performance and develop the business

- Conceptual and cognitive skills needed to think strategically, analyse information, solve problems and make decisions

- People skills, including those necessary to manage relationships with staff, colleagues and customers

- Personal effectiveness skills required to self-manage in the role.

## Standardisation and de-skilling

**3.73** This chapter has already recognised that not all trends in the labour market are moving in the direction of upskilling although, as previously stated, the weight of evidence suggests that across the economy the demand for higher levels of skill far outweighs the examples of jobs where skill needs have fallen.

**3.74** There are examples of de-skilling in insurance and banking. In insurance the automation of household and personal insurance services systems enables quotations to be provided by operatives who do not possess in-depth knowledge of insurance. Task range and variety in operator level jobs is small and discretion can only be used to a limited extent. However, the de-skilling that has occurred in these sectors has come about only partly as a result of automation. Many employers have chosen to use new technology as a means of delivering standardised policies and organising work, so that skill demands are polarised between the relatively low levels needed from clerks and higher levels of skill needed from senior underwriters (Rolfe, 1986).

**3.75** Call centres are often portrayed as modern day "dark satanic mills" where skill demands are minimal. This is overstated. Where the purpose of a call centre is to sell standardised products calling on minimal discretion by the job holder, skill demands will reflect this. However, in many call centres a wide range of skills are demanded including those skills needed by call centre operatives to do their job effectively. Case studies in the employers case study report on the banking sector found that:

*"Call centre staff need confidence in talking to customers and an ability to do that in a certain way (leading to a sale) and good organisational skills since there is still a lot of paperwork involved"* (Woodward et al, 2000)

Crome (1998) has observed that a lack of training of call centre staff to develop appropriate telephone communication and sales skills is undermining the effectiveness of many call centres.

**3.76** In food processing, many of the largest producers in this industry specialise in mass production of standardised products for which a great deal of the production process is now highly automated. This has tended to reduce craft skill requirements in production departments in recent decades. However, these firms require high-level and intermediate skills for product development, process engineering and marketing functions. In addition, the industry also embraces a number of specialist producers who are catering for higher value-added niche markets and whose production skill needs are correspondingly much greater than is the case for bulk producers.

# Summary

**3.77** There has been a broad shift in skill demand over the last 30 years away from skills related to manual work towards skills related to cognitive abilities. The shift in employment away from manual jobs towards non-manual jobs is a clear sign of this trend. The research based on more direct measures of skills show that it is generic skills such as communication, problems solving and the ability to use IT equipment which are rising in demand while the demand for skills related to manual strength and dexterity are falling . These trends are projected to continue.

**3.78** There has been a shift within intermediate level employment away from traditional skilled trade jobs towards associate professional jobs. This is part of the move from manual to non-manual work. However, there are more specific skills needed in the associate professional jobs being created in dynamic service sectors of the economy. These are skills related to creativity and design and the ability to translate ideas into a saleable product. Similar trends are apparent in professional occupations where job growth has expanded in dynamic service sectors such as public and financial and business services.

**3.79** While the overall numbers employed in skilled trade jobs have declined, the importance of these type of skilled workers to the productive sector has not. Jobs in skilled trades have declined in line with the overall reduction of employment in production jobs - this level of skill remains very important to industry. However, while still termed skilled trade, the type of work done is now far removed from traditional craft-type work. Greater emphasis on multi-skilling has broken down many traditional craft boundaries. The move to cellular and team working has resulted in more emphasis on multi-functioning, with craft workers expected to develop a range of generic skills to cope with this.

**3.80** There continues to be a significant number of job opportunities at lower levels, especially in jobs with fast labour turnover and high retirement rates. It is in these lower level jobs where the demand for higher levels of skills is least marked. However, the skill demands of these types of jobs are changing. These types of jobs are placing a much greater emphasis on communication and customer handling type skills. What is clear is that there are few job opportunities for those with minimal levels of skill.

**3.81** New technology and greater global competition are both driving up skill demands. The relationship between new technology, increased competition and skills is not monotonic, it depends very much on how employers organise work and make use of new technologies. The weight of evidence suggests that new technology, and particularly Information Technology, has led to a greater demand for workers who can solve problems and interpret information. It has led to a demand for people with an awareness of how systems (e.g. production systems) work and fit together. In striving for greater competitiveness, employers are emphasising both quality and costs. They are looking to achieve this by introducing a range of techniques and work practices that emphasis particular skills. Of particular importance in many workplaces is the ability to work as a team, to influence others and communicate effectively.

**3.82** Although the overwhelming trend is one of rising skill needs there are some jobs where skill requirements have fallen. Ironically, the causes are often similar to those that have raised the skills involved in other jobs. For example, international competition has induced some industries to introduce new technologies and ways of working which cut costs by standardising the product range and reducing workers' autonomy. This has meant that some workers need fewer and/or lower level skills. Nevertheless, the evidence presented in this chapter shows convincingly that examples of de-skilling are relatively small and few in number compared with the widespread and often considerable rise in skill levels demanded by many jobs.

**REFERENCES**

Adler, P., (1986a), "New Technologies, New Skills", *California Management Review* 29: 9-18.

Adler, P., (1986b), "Rethinking the Skill Requirements of New Technologies." In D. Whittington (ed.) *High Hopes for High Tech.* Chapel Hill, N.C.: University of North Carolina Press.

Allen, S. (1996), "Technology and the wage structure", Working paper 5534, Cambridge, MA: National Bureau of Economic Research.

Ashton, D., Davies, B., Felstead, A., Green, F., (1999) *Work Skills in Britain.* Oxford, SKOPE, Oxford and Warwick Universities.

Attewell, P. (1992), "Skill and Occupational Changes in US Manufacturing." in P.S. Adler ed *Technology and the Future of Work,* Oxford University Press. New York.

Autor, D., Katz, L. and Krueger, A. (1998), "Computing inequality: have computers changed the labor market?", *Quarterly Journal of Economics,* 113: 1269-1214.

Berman, E., Bound, J. and Machin, S. (1998), "Implications of skill-biased technological change: international evidence", *Quarterly Journal of Economics,* 113(4): 1245-1279.

Bound, J. and Johnson, G. (1992), "Changes in the structure of wages in the 1980's: an evaluation of alternative explanations", *American Economic Review,* 82(3): 371-392.

Bynner, J. (1994) "Skills and Occupations: Analysis of Cohort Members' Self-Reported Skills in the Fifth sweep of the National Child Development Study," NCDS User Support Group Working Paper 45, Social Statistics Research Group.

Bynner, J., Morphy, L. and Parsons, S. (1996) "Women, Employment and Skills," NCDS User Support Group Working Paper 44, Social Statistics Research Group.

Cappelli, P., Bassi, L., Katz, H., Knoke, D., Osterman, P., and Useem, M., (1997) *Change at Work,* Oxford University Press, Oxford, New York.

Caselli, F. (1999), "Technological Revolutions", *American Economic Review,* 89(1): 78-102.

Crome, M. (1998), "Call centres: battery farming or free range?" In *Industrial and Commercial Training* 30 (4): 137-141.

Cully, M., Woodward, S., O'Reilly, A., and Dix, G, (1999) *Britain at Work: As depicted by the 1998 Workplace Employee Relations Survey.* Routledge, London.

EMTA (1999), *Labour Market Survey of the Engineering Industry in Britain,* Watford: Engineering and Marine Training Authority.

Espinasse, J.M. and Vincens, J. (1997), "Les competences sur le marche du travail. Penurie ou plethore?", *TSER Project Working Paper,* LIRHE, University of Toulouse.

Felstead, A., Ashton, D., Green, F. (2000), "Are Britain's workplace skills becoming more unequal?", *Cambridge Journal of Economics,* (Forthcoming).

Finegold, D and Wagner, L (1999), "The German Skill-Creation System and Team-Based Production: Competitive Asset or Liability?", in P.D. Culpepper and D. Finegold eds *The German Skills Machine - Sustaining Comparative Advantage in a Global Economy.* Berghahn Books. New York.

Gallie, D. (1991), "Patterns of skill change: upskilling, deskilling or the polarization of skills?" *Work, Employment and Society* 5 (3 September): 319:351.

Gallie, D. and White, M. (1993), *Employee Commitment and the Skills Revolution.* London, PSI Publishing.

Giles, L., La Valle, I., and Perryman, S. (1996), *A New Deal for Secretaries?* IES Report 313.

Giret, J.F. and Masjuan, J.M. (1999), "The diffusion of qualifications in the Spanish labour market", *Journal of Education and Work* 12 (2): 179-199.

Green, F., D. Ashton, B. Burchell, B. Davies and A. Felstead (2000). "Are British Workers Getting More Skilled? *The Over-Educated Worker?*" in L. Borghans and A. de Grip (eds.) *The Economics of Skill Utilisation.* Cheltenham, Edward Elgar.

Green, F. (1999), *The market value of generic skills,* National Skills Task Force Research Paper 8, September.

Green, F., Felstead, A. and Gallie, D. (1999), "Computers are even more important than you thought: an analysis of the changing skill-intensity of jobs", Paper presented to EEEG Annual Conference, July 1999.

Haskel, J. and Heden, Y. (1999), "Computers and the demand for skilled labour: industry and establishment-level panel evidence for the UK", *Economic Journal,* 109: C68-C79.

Hasluck, C. (2000), Special report on replacement demand in the computer services industry produced for the Department for Education and Employment (Unpublished).

Hendry, C, Woodward, S, Brown, A., Christodoulou, K, Brown, J, Rowley, C, Alport, E, Holtham, C, Courtney, N, Spedale, S, (2000) *The Extent, Causes and Implications of Skills Deficiencies in the UK Telecommunications Sector,* Skills Task Force Case Study Research Paper.

Hendry, C. (1999), *New Technology Industries,* National Skills Task Force Research Paper 10, September.

Hirschhorn, L., (1984) *Beyond Mechanization: Work and Technology in a Postindustrial Age.* Cambridge, Mass: MIT Press.

ITNTO (1999), *Skills 99: IT Skills Summary.* Report to the Department of Trade and Industry.

Katz, L. and Murphy, K. (1992), "Changes in Relative Wages, 1963-1987: Supply and Demand Factors", *Quarterly Journal of Economics,* 107: 35-78.

Keep, E. and Mayhew, K. (1998), "Was Ratner Right? Product market and competitive strategies and their links with skills and knowledge". *Employment Policy Institute Economic Report* Vol 12 No 3: pp1-14.

Kettley, P and Strebler, M. (1997), *Changing Roles for Senior Managers,* IES Report No 327.

Krueger, A. (1993), "How computers have changed the wage structure - evidence from microdata, 1984-1989", *Quarterly Journal of Economics,* 108: 33-60.

Lloyd, C. (1997), 'Microelectronics in the clothing industry: firm strategy and the skills debate." *New Technology, Work and Employment* 12(1): 36-47.

Lyons, B. and Bailey, S. (1993), "Small subcontractors in UK engineering: competitiveness, dependence and problems", *Small Business Economics,* 5: 101-109.

Machin, S. (1996), "Changes in the relative demand for skills in the UK labour market", in A. Booth, D. Snower (eds), *Acquiring Skills: Market Failures, their Symptoms and Policy Responses,* Cambridge: Cambridge University Press.

Mason, G. (1999a), *Engineering skills formation in Britain: cyclical and structural issues,* National Skills Task Force Research Paper 7, September.

Mason, G. (1999b), *The labour market for technical graduates: are there mismatches between supply and demand?,* Research Report 112, Department for Education and Employment.

Mason, G. (1999c), "Product strategies, workforce skills and 'high-involvement' work practices", in P. Cappelli (ed.), *Employment Practices and Business Strategy,* New York: Oxford University Press.

O'Farrell, P. and Oakey, R. (1993), "The employment and skill implications of the adoption of new technology: a comparison of small engineering firms in core and peripheral regions", *Urban Studies,* 30 (3): 507-526.

Robinson, P. and Manacorda, M. (1997), *Qualifications and the labour market in Britain: 1984-94 skill biased change in demand for labour or credentialism?,* LSE, Centre for Economic Performance, Discussion Paper No. 330. February.

Rolfe, H. (1986), "Skill, de-skilling and new technology in the non-manual labour process", *New Technology, Work and Employment,* volume 1, number 1.

Rowley, G, Purcell, K, Richardson, M, Shackleton, R, Howe, S and Whitley, P (2000) *The Extent, Causes and Implications of Skills Deficiencies in the hotel and catering sector,* Skills Task Force Case Study Research Paper.

Senker, P. J. (1992), "Automation and Work in Britain" in P.S. Adler (ed) *Technology and the Future of Work,* Oxford University Press. New York.

Steedman, H. (1999), "Diplomas versus skills", *European Journal of Vocational Training,* Number 16, Jan-Apr 1999/1, CEDEFOP.

Steedman, H, Mason, G, and Wagner, K. (1991) "Intermediate Skills in the Workplace: Deployment, Standards and Supply in Britain, France and Germany.", *National Institute Economic Review,* 136: 60-76.

Thompson, P., Wallace, T., Flecker, J., and Ahlstrand, R. (1995) "It ain't what you do, it's the way that you do it: Production organisation and skill utilisation in commercial vehicles". *Work, Employment and Society* 9(4): 719-741.

Waterson, P., Clegg, C. W., Bolden, R., Pepper, K., Warr, P.B., & Wall, T.D., (1999), "The use and effectiveness of modern manufacturing practices: A survey of UK industry". *International Journal of Production Research,* 37, 2271-2292.

Wood, A. (1995), "How trade hurt unskilled workers", *Journal of Economic Perspectives,* 9(3): 57-80.

Woodward, S., Hendry, C., Alport, E., Harvey Cook, J., Vielba, C.A., Dobson, P. and Hockaday, N.(2000), *The Extent Causes and Implications of Skills Deficiencies - Sector Report for Banking, Finance and Insurance.* Skills Task Force Case Study Research Report.

Wilson, R.A. ed (2000), *Projections of Occupations and Qualifications,* IER.

# CHAPTER 4
## QUALIFICATIONS OF THE WORKFORCE AND JOB-RELATED SKILLS

## Introduction

**4.1**   The demand for skilled workers is growing as shifts in occupational structure, the introduction of new technology, IT and new work practices raise the average level of skill needed in the average job. The implications of an inadequate or inappropriate supply of skills are considerable and wide ranging. They include: lower profits for firms, lower wages for individuals and slower economic growth. This chapter reviews the evidence on the skills available to employers in the UK. It describes what progress has been made, identifies where the current supply of skills may be inadequate and assesses whether current trends in education and training will help improve skills in these areas.

**4.2**   The chapter starts by describing the growth in the proportion of the labour force possessing qualifications. It examines how the types and levels of qualifications held have changed. This leads to a discussion of areas where the current supply of skills may be insufficient to meet the needs of employers.

**4.3**   One of the major causes of the rise in qualification levels amongst the workforce has been the rising participation and attainment in formal education by young people which the chapter goes on to explore. It is noted that rising participation and attainment by young people has occurred at a time when the numbers of young people have been declining. In spite of rising rates of attainment, the UK continues to lag behind our international competitors in terms of the proportion of young people qualified to intermediate levels. This is particularly true for those vocationally qualified at this level and especially true for those qualified in technical disciplines.

**4.4**   The large expansion in Higher Education, which has contributed considerably to the growth in attainment is considered separately. Higher Education has contributed considerably to the growth in attainment. More recently the numbers graduating from relatively new courses with a clear vocational element have expanded much more rapidly than has the output from many of the more traditional subjects. These subjects include: computing, business and management, and design. We note that during the last few years there have been falls in the numbers graduating from some technical subjects like general engineering, physics and mathematics.

**4.5**   The penultimate part of the chapter considers whether workplace learning is helping to address the problem of relatively low levels of skill among the workforce. It looks at whether workplace learning is bridging the skills gap faced by many adults and concludes that it is not, mainly because the least qualified tend to receive little training. The chapter concludes by considering what impact future supply may have on the stock of skills and summarises the main themes and conclusions.

# The relationship between skills and qualifications

**4.6**   The analysis relies heavily on qualification levels as a proxy indicator for skills.  There are several problems associated with this approach.  Many qualifications, particularly general or academic qualifications, measure educational attainment rather than skills.  Many generic skills and personal attributes are not certified.  Consequently, it is problematic to estimate the supply of skills such as communication and interpersonal skills.

**4.7**   Skill levels are likely to be under estimated because a large proportion of learning does not lead to recognised qualifications.  The International Adult Learning Survey (1997) found that only around two-fifths of taught learning episodes were designed to lead to a qualification.  Learning episodes which do not lead to qualifications include formal and informal learning, and training which may take place on or off-the-job.  The outcome of these other routes to skills acquisition, particularly on-the-job informal training, is difficult to measure.  Nevertheless it is recognised that their contribution is both important and considerable.

**4.8**   The information on qualifications which exists often relates to the highest level of qualification held.  This approach underestimates the incidence of qualifications since people with higher level qualifications often have other qualifications which go unrecorded.

**4.9**   A common but difficult distinction to make is between academic or general qualifications and 'vocational' (work-related or job-related) qualifications.  This distinction is often arbitrary since many people enter occupations unrelated to the subject in which they have a qualification.  Nevertheless, there is still some value in trying to make the distinction as it provides some insight into the overall balance of qualifications held.

**4.10**  Despite these problems, qualifications data arguably provide some of the most useful indicators of trends in skills supply because of their detailed availability.  This data is the best proxy for skills when seeking to identify the economic returns to skills.  Qualifications data may also be an increasingly accurate measure as the emphasis increasingly is not just on having the skills needed to do a job but on achieving qualifications that attest to those skills and thus make them transferable.

## Rising qualification levels in the labour force

**4.11**  During the last twenty years the labour force has grown from just over 25 million in 1979 to around 28$^1/_2$ million in 1999.  The fact that those entering the labour market have been better qualified than those leaving it has contributed to a significant increase in the general qualification level of the workforce.  It is rising attainment amongst predominantly young people, that has produced these improvements.  Increases in the qualification levels of older employees in the labour market have been far more modest.

**4.12**  However, this increase in qualification levels is not as large as may be perceived by simply looking at the increased rate of young people gaining qualifications.  The numbers of 16-19 year olds in the population fell from just over 3,400 in 1988 to just over 2,900 in 1999.  While the <u>number</u> of 16-19 year olds qualified to Level 2 or above grew by 40% this is a smaller rise than the <u>proportion</u> of 16-19 year olds qualifying to Level 2 - which grew by over 60% (from 39% in 1988 to nearly 64% in 1999).

**4.13** Figure 4.1 shows that the proportion of the workforce holding formal qualifications increased from just over half in 1979 to almost nine in ten in 1999. The proportion of the workforce holding qualifications equivalent to NVQ Level 4 or above has more than doubled since 1979 and a quarter of the workforce is now qualified to this level. One fifth of economically active people have their highest qualifications at NVQ Level 3 or equivalent with just over half (56%) having qualifications at Level two or below.

**Figure 4.1: Qualification levels of economically active people of working age[1] (UK)**

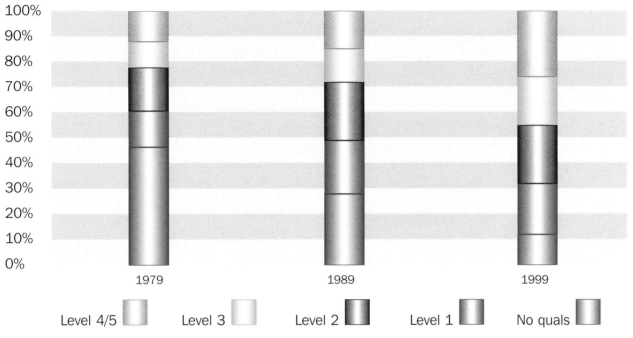

Source: LFS[2]

## Gaps in vocational attainment and at the intermediate level

**4.14** Although qualification levels in the UK are rising there are significant differences in the type of qualifications held (Table 4.1). In 1999 over half of all those in employment had general qualifications and under one-third held vocational qualifications as their highest qualification. The Task Force commented in its earlier reports its concern that people who have acquired only general qualifications may not have had the opportunity to develop the vocational skills needed in the labour market.[3][4]

---

[1] 16-64 years old for males and 16-59 for females.

[2] There have been many changes to the LFS between 1979 and 1999 and it is not possible to calculate the effect of all these changes on qualifications data. The data for the years shown are not directly comparable but they are indicative of the extent to which qualifications of different types and levels have become more common throughout the population. See Annex 1 for definition of which qualifications are allocated to which level.

[3] Second Report of the National Skills Task Force - Delivering Skills For All

[4] Academic or general qualifications are defined as degrees, higher degrees, other degrees, diploma in Higher Education, Higher Education below degree, A-level, Scottish CSYS, SCE higher, AS level, O-level/GCSE/CSE. Vocational qualifications include all other qualifications recorded by the LFS (professional qualifications, HNC, HND, BTEC, OND, ONC, City and Guilds, SCOTVEC, teaching and nursing qualifications, RSAs, NVQs, GNVQs and YT).

**4.15** The lowest qualified are much more likely to hold a general qualification as their highest qualification and less likely to hold a vocational qualification as their highest qualification than the better qualified.  Of those qualified below NVQ Level 3 in 1999 less than 20% held a vocational qualification as their highest.  Perhaps this is not surprising given that research shows that the returns to vocational qualifications at Levels 1 and 2 are very small (Dearden et al, 2000).  As discussed later in this chapter the low numbers with vocational qualifications at this level compares unfavourably with some of our international competitors.

**Table 4.1: Trends in types and levels of qualifications held by those in employment (UK)**

| | 1979 | 1989 | 1999 |
|---|---|---|---|
| Degree and above | 11% | 13% | 20% |
| General Level 4 below degree | 0% | 0% | 2% |
| Vocational Level 4 below degree | 2% | 3% | 4% |
| General Level 3 | 3% | 4% | 6% |
| Vocational Level 3 | 7% | 8% | 13% |
| Other Level 3 | - | 1% | 1% |
| General Level 2 | 9% | 13% | 12% |
| Vocational Level 2 | 7% | 8% | 9% |
| Other Level 2 | 1% | 2% | 3% |
| General Level 1 | 10% | 12% | 14% |
| Vocational Level 1 | 3% | 5% | 2% |
| Other Level 1 | 2% | 4% | 4% |
| No qualifications | 45% | 27% | 12% |

Source: LFS[2]

**4.16** More, and a growing proportion, of those qualified at NVQ Level 3 and above hold vocational qualifications.  However, these qualifications tend to be concentrated at NVQ Level 4 and above.  In 1999 only just over one in ten of those in jobs held a Level 3 vocational qualification as their highest qualification.

**4.17** The UK deficit in vocational qualifications at Levels two and three is clear when compared with our main competitors.  As we can see in Table 4.2, despite the improvements in the qualification levels of the UK workforce referred to above, the UK still has one-third fewer people qualified to NVQ Level 2 than either France or Germany and only half as many people qualified to NVQ Level 3 or above than is the case in Germany.  While comparisons of qualification levels between countries need to be treated with caution because of differences in education and training systems, Table 4.2 also makes it clear that the main reasons for this deficit, at least when compared to Germany, is the lower proportion of the UK workforce with intermediate level vocational qualifications - the UK compares favourably on the proportions with general education qualifications.

**Table 4.2: Comparisons of qualifications at Level 2+ and 3+ in the UK, France and Germany**

| | Level 2+ | | | Level 3+ | | |
|---|---|---|---|---|---|---|
| | **UK** | **France** | **Germany** | **UK** | **France** | **Germany** |
| | **1998** | **1998** | **1997**[2] | **1998** | **1998** | **1997**[2] |
| 19-21 year olds, general education | 44% | 56% | 37% | 29% | 38% | 22% |
| 19-21 year olds, vocational | 26% | 25% | 28% | 14% | 5% | 26% |
| 19-21 year olds, total | **70%** | **81%** | **65%** | **43%** | **43%** | **48%** |
| 25-28 year olds, general education | 33% | 40% | 33% | 24% | 36% | 30% |
| 25-28 year olds, vocational | 28% | 43% | 52% | 17% | 18% | 48% |
| 25-28 year olds, total | **61%** | **83%** | **85%** | **41%** | **54%** | **78%** |
| Workforce[1], general education | 27% | 31% | 25% | 20% | 25% | 22% |
| Workforce[1], vocational | 27% | 41% | 58% | 17% | 12% | 52% |
| Workforce[1], total | **55%** | **73%** | **83%** | **37%** | **36%** | **74%** |

[1] Aged 16-64 (UK women aged 16-59)                    Source: Steedman (1999)

[2] Former Bundesrepublik (FRG)

See annex 2 for definition of which qualifications are defined at which level

## The long tail of low qualifications and the high incidence of poor basic skills

**4.18** The large growth in educational attainment has led to a rapid decline in the proportion of the labour force without qualifications. In 1979 nearly half of the workforce had no qualifications compared to just over one in ten in 1999. Nevertheless, the majority of the workforce still have either low level[5] or no qualifications. Furthermore, given that much of the growth in qualifications is due to rising participation and attainment amongst young people, it is not surprising that the likelihood of holding qualifications falls with age. A 50-59 year old is almost four times as likely and a 40-49 year old just over twice as likely to possess no formal qualifications than a 20-29 year old.

**4.19** We should not assume that poor qualification levels necessarily mean poor basic skills. Though basic skills are positively associated with the highest level of qualification held, there are some people with low qualifications who have relatively good basic skills and others with high qualifications who have relatively poor basic skills. For example, the International Adult Literacy Survey (IALS) found that around 15% of people with Higher Education degree level qualifications had literacy skills below Level three whilst nearly two fifths of the unqualified had literacy skills at Level three or above[6]. Nevertheless there is a strong correlation between poor basic skills and poor qualifications.

---

[5] At Level two or below.

[6] Level 3 literacy level on the prose test requires the reader to match information requiring low level inferences or that meet specific conditions. There may be several pieces of information to be identified located in different parts of the text. Readers may also be required to compare and contrast information. (Carey et al, 1997)

**4.20** It is now widely accepted that a significant proportion of adults in the UK have poor basic skills (Moser, 1999). At the same time, the general upskilling occurring in many jobs means that basic skills are becoming more important in more jobs. Research suggests that almost every job, even in lower occupational categories (e.g. below professional/technical level), now requires some competence in basic skills and that, as such, 50% of jobs are closed to people who only have Entry Level basic skills (IES, 1993).

**4.21** Seven million adults in England - one in five adults - are functionally illiterate. This means they have a lower literacy level than is expected of an eleven year old child. Research by the Centre of Longitudinal Studies for the Basic Skills Agency found that 6% of the adult working population are judged to have "very low" literacy skills and a further 13% to have "low" literacy skills. Individuals with "very low" literacy skills have great difficulty with any reading and struggle to read the shortest and simplest texts. People with "low" literacy skills may be able to read short articles in tabloid newspapers but would be unable to find details for plumbers in the Yellow Pages (low literacy skills are the equivalent of NVQ Level 1).

**4.22** Problems with numeracy skills are even worse. Some researchers estimate that nearly half of all adults in the UK have numeracy skills below the level expected of an eleven year old and a quarter have 'very low' numeracy skills. Those with 'very low' numeracy skills are unable to perform even the simplest of calculations. Individuals with "low" numeracy skills can cope with simple transactions but find percentages and fractions difficult. One third of adults could not calculate the area of a room that was 21ft by 14 ft even with the use of a calculator.

**4.23** The extent of poor basic skills in the UK can be seen when we compare ourselves with other countries. IALS (1997) found that only two of the twelve participating countries had a higher proportion of adults than Britain with low levels of literacy and numeracy. For example, figure 4.2 shows that only Ireland and Poland had a larger proportion of adults than the UK with document literacy at below Level 3.

**Figure 4.2: Percentage of adult population aged 16-65 at document literacy level 1994/95 in selected countries**

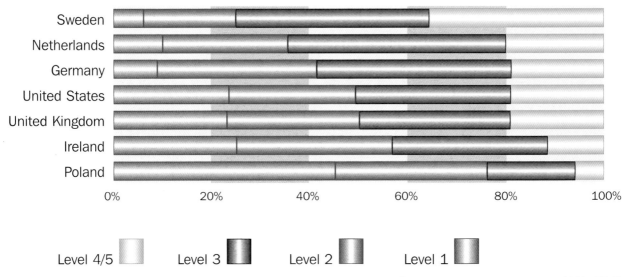

Source: Adult Literacy in Britain 1997 (IALS)

**4.24** People with lower levels of literacy are less likely to engage in adult education and training. Thus, the less literate will have fewer opportunities to upgrade their skills. Since only 7% of people at the lowest document literacy level assessed themselves as having poor reading skills and nearly two-thirds of people with low document literacy skills believed they had *good* or *excellent* reading skills they are unlikely to feel the need to upgrade their existing skills.

**4.25** Overall, the evidence suggests that the low skill levels associated with having a large number of adults with low level or no qualifications are only part of the problem. In particular, many people, mainly but not exclusively those with low levels of educational attainment, have poor basic skills. This is likely to create problems for employers who increasingly require workers with the ability to read and write at a good level. It also creates problems for the individuals themselves who are likely to find it difficult to acquire other skills and qualifications without first improving their basic skills.

## Increased participation and attainment in general education

**4.26** It was discussed earlier how the qualification level of new entrants to the labour market has been a major factor in raising the qualifications held by the labour force as a whole. In 1988 30% of 16-19 year olds were qualified to Level 2 with a further 8% qualified to Level 3. By 1999 42% of 16-19 year olds were qualified to Level 2 with a further 21% qualified at Level 3. However, it was also noted how this needs to be set in the context of demographic changes.

**4.27** A major contributing factor to the increase in qualification levels of new entrants to the labour market has been the rise in qualification achieved before completing compulsory education. During the last decade attainment amongst fifteen year olds taking GCSEs and GNVQs (or equivalents) has increased. Figure 4.3 shows that the percentage of pupils achieving 5 or more GCSE grades A* to C has risen from around one-third of 15 year olds at the end of the 1980s to the current level where nearly half of 15 year olds gain this level of qualification before reaching school leaving age.

**Figure 4.3: Percentage of pupils aged 15 in schools achieving 5 or more GCSEs A* - C, England 1988/89 to 1998/99 (Provisional)**

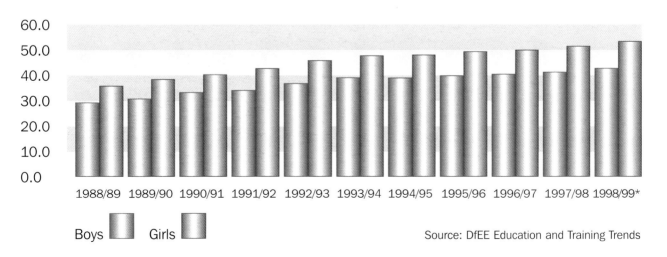

Source: DfEE Education and Training Trends

**4.28** In 1988 eight in ten 16 year olds and nearly seven in ten 17 year olds participated in some form of education and training. By 1998 this had increased by ten percentage points for each age group - to nine in ten 16 year olds and eight in ten seventeen year olds. This rise in participation has contributed to the increase in qualifications achieved by 16-18 year olds. However, a more significant contribution has come from the different method of participation and the level of qualification studied by those undertaking post-compulsory education and training.

**4.29** In 1988 around two-thirds of 16 and 17 year olds undertaking some form of education and training were in full-time education. By 1998 some four in five 16-17 year olds receiving education and training were doing so on a full-time basis. This shift towards full-time education has been accompanied by an increase in the level of qualification studied. In 1988 21% of 16 year olds in education were on a course leading to a Level 1 or 2 qualification while 30% were on a course leading to a Level 3 qualification. By 1998 22% of 16 year olds in education were on a course leading to a Level 1 or 2 qualification while 48% were on a course leading to a Level 3 qualification.

**4.30** Before going on to consider how young people have acquired these higher levels of qualification, we should acknowledge that this paper focuses almost exclusively on the national picture. This obscures some important geographical variations. For example, rates of participation in full-time post-compulsory education vary significantly between regions. In 1996/97 participation rates for 16 year olds varied from 71% in the North East to 81% in the South West. Sub-regional and local differences tend to be even greater. This variation leads to differences in attainment and subsequent learning which in turn lead to differences in the supply of qualifications available to employers in different parts of the UK. There is not scope to do full justice to the regional and sub-regional dimension of skills supply in this chapter. However, it is an important issue, particularly when assessing the balance between the demand and supply of skills.

**Higher attainment at Levels 2 & 3 but limited growth in the vocationally qualified**

**4.31** The most significant contribution to the achievement of Level 3 qualifications by young people comes from those taking GCE A-levels. Just over half of young people gain a Level 3 qualification by age 21. Of these 60% do so through gaining 2 GCE A-levels.

**4.32** Just over one-third of seventeen year olds reached NVQ Level 3 in 1998/9, almost double the percentage that achieved this 10 years earlier. This significant increase in the numbers of young people gaining qualifications at Levels 2 and 3 means that relative to France and Germany the UK performance is much improved to that shown in the 1996 Skills Audit (DfEE/Cabinet Office, 1996). Indeed the proportion of UK 19-21 year olds with this level of qualification is now comparable with France and Germany (see Table 4.2). However, the apparent progress made by the UK in the qualification levels of 19-21 year olds, reflected in Table 4.2, is in many ways misleading.

**4.33** Young people in continental Europe take longer to gain qualifications - particularly vocational qualifications than in the UK. The participation rate for 19 year olds in ISCED 3 (upper secondary education) was 16% for the UK in 1995/6 compared to 32% for the EU-15 average (European Commission, 1998).

**4.34** Overall therefore, while progress has been made in raising the qualification level of new entrants to the UK labour market, we still lag a long way behind international competitors such as Germany when we allow for differences in education and training systems. Looking at the more comparable 25-28 age group in Table 4.2, there is a considerable gap between the UK and France, and more so between the UK and Germany in the proportion of this age group with Level 2 and Level 3 qualifications. Furthermore, the UK also faces a significant gap with some non-European countries - over 90% of 25-28 year olds in Korea and Japan are qualified to Level 3 or above.

**4.35** The gap in qualification levels between the UK and France and Germany is particularly significant if we focus on vocational qualifications where Germany has double the proportion of 25-28 year olds at Level 2 and treble the proportion at Level 3 compared with the UK (Table 4.2). However, significant numbers of the UK population do acquire Level 2 and Level 3 vocational qualifications after reaching the age of 25. Latest National Information System for Vocational Qualifications (NISVQ) data shows that of the 300,000 Level 2 vocational qualifications recorded[7] by NISVQ in 1998/9, 45% were achieved by those aged 25 or older. Similarly of the 150,000 Level 3 vocational qualifications recorded, 42% were achieved by those aged 25 or older (DfEE, 2000). Together this still only represents just 1% of the working age population over the age of 25.

**4.36** The expansion in qualifications in the UK has occurred to a greater extent in some disciplines and subjects compared to others. Most of the growth in GCE A-level holders has been for those taking relatively new subjects such as computing, communication studies and business studies. The growth in more traditional subjects like maths, chemistry and physics has been subdued in comparison and indeed entries in physics actually fell during the 1990s. Steedman et al (2000) found that the UK has a much smaller supply of individuals who have studied advanced mathematics and physics at age 16, than other countries (France, Germany, US and Singapore were the other countries considered). The same story emerges for GNVQs and NVQs - 57% of all Advanced GNVQs awarded in 1997/98 were for the business version of the qualification and of the 458,000 NVQ/SVQs awarded in 1997/8 fewer than 100,000 of these were in technical disciplines such as construction, engineering, manufacturing or chemicals (and only 18,000 of these were at Level 3 or higher).

**4.37** An important reason for this seems to be that the basis for studying disciplines requiring a mathematical background is not being developed among young people before they complete their compulsory education. Too few acquire good levels of qualification in mathematics. Just 45% of 15 year olds gain a grade C in GCSE mathematics. Less than 10% of the cohort go on to take GCE A-level maths. This is a very limited pool of people with the basic building block on which more advanced technical skills can be built.

---

[7] The NISVQ recorded 90% of all NVQs awarded in 1998/9. It also collects the other vocational qualifications awarded by the four largest awarding bodies: City and Guilds, Edexcel (formerly BTEC), OCR (formerly RSA) and SQA.

## Sharp growth in Higher Education

**4.38** The contribution to increased qualification levels provided by post-compulsory education at age 16-18 has been matched by that provided by higher education.  The proportion of young people entering Higher Education has risen sharply (see figure 4.4).  Since 1994 around one in three young people have entered Higher Education in England compared with one in six in 1989 and one in eighteen during the early 1960s.  The UK's net entry rate[8], in 1996, to university level education was well above the OECD average.  At 41%, we were well ahead of Germany (27%) though behind countries such as Japan and Singapore.

**Figure 4.4: Participation by young people in Higher Education, Age Participation Index (API), Great Britain, 1984/85 to 1998/99**

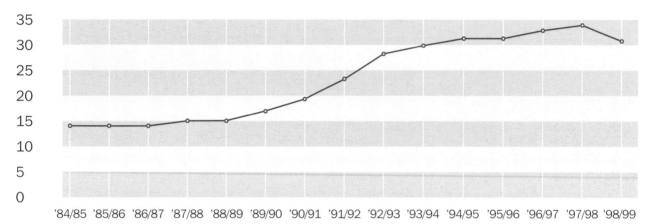

Source: DfEE Education and Training Trends

(1) The API measures the number of home domiciled young (aged under 21) initial entrants to full-time and sandwich undergraduate courses, expressed as a proportion of the average 18 to 19 year old Great Britain population.

**4.39** This increase in participation has been quite evenly shared amongst full-time and part-time students with numbers almost doubling for both between 1987/88 and 1997/98.  The number of part-time students has increased most rapidly since 1993/94.  Another feature of the growth in Higher Education participation over the last 15 years has been the rapid growth in mature entrants where growth rates have been nearly treble that achieved by younger students.

**4.40** Rising admissions are translating into similarly large increases in the number of people gaining Higher Education qualifications.  The number of Higher Education qualifications awarded in Higher Education institutions in England more than doubled between 1987/88 and 1994/95, since when they have continued to increase steadily.

---

[8] Entry rates to Higher Education estimate the percentage of school leavers who will enter Higher Education at some stage in their lives, given current conditions.

## Expansion in "new" vocational subjects

**4.41** Not all disciplines have shared equally in the Higher Education expansion. The fastest growth in first degree graduates has taken place in relatively modern subjects such as design studies, communication studies, computing, marketing and business[9]. Many of these subjects have a clear vocational element. The growth in more traditional subjects has been relatively subdued or even negative. Notably, the numbers gaining qualifications in many engineering disciplines, physical sciences, maths and building/architecture have fallen. The decline in physics and some engineering courses (civil and combined engineering) went hand in hand with the rapid expansion of Higher Education in the late 1980s and early 1990s.

**Table 4.3: Higher Education first degree attainment in selected subjects in 1998 and change since 1994/95**

|  | Numbers obtaining 1st degree 1998 | Change 1994/5-1997/8 |
| --- | --- | --- |
| **"New" Vocational Subjects** | | |
| Communication studies | 1309 | 33% |
| Design studies | 9633 | 32% |
| Business & management studies | 17323 | 12% |
| Computer studies | 9991 | 21% |
| **"Traditional" Vocational Subjects** | | |
| Mechanical engineering | 3913 | 13% |
| Electrical engineering | 1014 | -16% |
| Electronic engineering | 3853 | 7% |
| Production/manufacturing engineering | 2332 | 7% |
| General engineering | 2245 | -12% |
| Building/construction | 3759 | -14% |
| **Academic Subjects** | | |
| History | 5562 | 4% |
| Mathematics | 3372 | -2% |
| Physics | 2320 | -6% |

Source: HESA

**4.42** Figures on registrations for sub-degree qualifications are difficult to compile. Table 4.4, which is based on EdExcel figures suggest the growth in sub-degree qualifications (HNC/HND) has been slower than the growth in first degrees. However, there are likely to be registrations on HNC/HND and other sub-degree courses not included in this data. The overall picture at sub-degree level suggests a general shift towards degree-level study by many people who in earlier generations might have sought sub-degree (technician-level) qualifications. As with degree level qualifications fastest growth has been in "new" vocational subjects such as IT. We remark below on the fall in the numbers acquiring sub-degree qualifications in engineering related subjects.

[9] Data on attainment by subject is available on a consistent basis between 1985-1993 and since 1994/95. This analysis focuses on the most recent period but highlights significant similarities and differences between the two periods.

**Table 4.4: Number of registrations by subject area on HNC and HND courses 1989/90 to 1998/9**

| Subject | 1989/90 | | | 1995/6 | | | 1998/9 | | |
|---|---|---|---|---|---|---|---|---|---|
| | HNC | HND | TOT | HNC | HND | TOT | HNC | HND | TOT |
| Art & Design | 260 | 4485 | 4745 | 683 | 5657 | 6300 | 1394 | 4767 | 6161 |
| Business & Management | 8106 | 7800 | 15906 | 10414 | 13227 | 23641 | 7709 | 10536 | 18245 |
| Construction & Built Env. | 6649 | 1825 | 8474 | 2985 | 2642 | 5627 | 2930 | 1495 | 4425 |
| Engineering/Tech & Manuf. | 13005 | 4854 | 26333 | 7898 | 7450 | 15348 | 8553 | 6477 | 15030 |
| Science/Health/Social Care | 2935 | 1818 | 4753 | 2372 | 3562 | 5934 | 3076 | 4052 | 7128 |
| Hospitality/Leisure | 174 | 1969 | 2143 | 474 | 5635 | 6109 | 545 | 3932 | 11605 |
| Land & Countryside | 45 | 550 | 495 | 298 | 1604 | 1902 | 603 | 1480 | 2083 |
| Media Communications | 0 | 0 | 0 | 118 | 2025 | 2143 | 464 | 2112 | 2576 |
| Sales | 0 | 0 | 0 | 38 | 18 | 56 | 21 | 1 | 22 |
| Information Technology | 2067 | 4249 | 6316 | 4119 | 6722 | 10841 | 5639 | 7459 | 13098 |
| **Total** | 33241 | 27550 | 60791 | 29399 | 48546 | 77945 | 30934 | 42338 | 73272 |

Source: EdExcel

### Decline in traditional technical disciplines

**4.43** In recent years there has been much concern about the supply of engineering graduates. Admissions to first degree engineering courses in Higher Education rose much more slowly than in many other subjects during the period of rapid expansion and have now started to decline. However, international comparisons suggest that the UK Higher Education system produces a similar proportion of graduate engineers compared with other developed countries (e.g. US and France) though considerably fewer than Germany and Japan (both of whom have much bigger manufacturing sectors). The labour market continues to signify a robust demand for these skills. While average graduate wages did not increase above the rate of inflation during the 1990s the relative return to engineering degrees did increase at a rate of about 1.5% above inflation (Vignoles and Hansen, 2000).

**4.44** The biggest shortfall in the UK appears to occur at sub-degree level where historically the numbers taking engineering is far lower than in Germany, France and Singapore (Steedman et al, 2000). Table 4.4 suggests that the numbers taking these courses in the UK in the last 10 years has fallen significantly.

**4.45** Expanding Higher Education places in engineering is unlikely to be an option in the UK because of the lack of suitably qualified applicants. A-level attainment in mathematics and physics are often pre-requisites for engineering courses.[10] The limited pool of people gaining these qualifications has been discussed earlier and recent research suggests that the number of students eligible to take engineering courses in Higher Education has barely increased during the 1990s (Hansen and Vignoles 1999). This is primarily due to the fall in the number of those gaining A-level physics during this time and is of particular concern in the case of electronic engineering, a subject area which has featured strongly in recent reports of recruitment difficulties (Mason, 1999).

---

[10] However, this is changing with around one-third of engineering entrants in the UK being admitted with qualifications other than A-levels.

**4.46** It has been suggested that the quality of engineering entrants may be a problem for the UK. The evidence on this is mixed. The mean A-level scores of those entering engineering have in fact risen faster than average and the top engineering courses attract many entrants with good A-level grades. However, at the other end of the spectrum, there are some engineering degree courses which can only fill places with very modest A-level entry requirements (Mason, 1999).[11]

### Dispersion of graduates through the labour market

**4.47** As the supply of graduates has increased they have taken up a wider range of jobs in the labour market. In 1981 over 60% of graduates in the labour market were in professional jobs. By 1998 less than 50% of graduates in the labour market were in these types of jobs. However, this dispersion of graduates through the labour market has been limited and over 90% of graduates are to be found in managerial, professional and associate professional jobs, as was the case in 1981.

**Table 4.5: Graduate penetration by occupation (% qualified at degree level or above)**

| SOC 1990 Sub-Major Groups (selected) | % of those in employment with First or Higher Degree | | |
|---|---|---|---|
| | **1981** | **1998** | **2009 (projection)** |
| Corporate Administrators | 12.9 | 30.6 | 41.0 |
| Managers & Proprietors | 3.1 | 8.4 | 11.5 |
| Science & Engineering Professionals | 43.0 | 50.8 | 56.6 |
| Health Professionals | 95.8 | 97.4 | 97.2 |
| Teaching Professionals | 59.9 | 77.5 | 84.1 |
| Other Professionals | 60.8 | 71.7 | 76.7 |
| Science Associate Professionals | 16.2 | 25.3 | 26.5 |
| Health Associate Professionals | 3.0 | 11.5 | 16.1 |
| Other Associate Professionals | 16.7 | 27.1 | 33.0 |
| Buyers, Brokers and Sales Reps* | 5.4 | 10.5 | 14.0 |

*included because in new SOC 2000 classification most of these jobs are classified as Associate Professional

Source: Wilson, (2000)

**4.48** Many more graduates are now entering managerial and associate professional jobs than was the case in the past and over one fifth of those in these occupations are now graduates. This trend of increased graduate penetration into these occupations is expected to continue and by 2009 33% of managers and 27% of associate professionals are expected to be graduates (Table 4.5). Further penetration of graduates into these jobs can be expected after then as more non-graduates retire from the labour force.

[11] Note that roughly a third of all entrants to UK engineering degree courses now hold qualifications other than A-levels or Scottish Highers.

**4.49** We would have expected more managerial jobs to be filled by graduates as a result of the expansion in Higher Education during the 1980s and 1990s. The low proportion of UK managers who were graduates (only just over one in ten UK managers were graduates in 1981) compared unfavourably with many of our international competitors. Employers were always likely to seek to tap into this growing pool of talent.

**4.50** The growing proportion of graduates entering associate professional jobs reflects both the demise of traditional vocational routes into these jobs and the growth of new jobs in these areas (e.g. business service and IT) which are biased towards graduate-level entry. Research suggests there may be drawbacks to the recruitment of graduates to these types of jobs. Concerns about the quality of graduates applying for technical jobs have been highlighted in a number of surveys (Mason, 2000). The quality lacking usually refers to a lack of work experience, commercial understanding and generic skills. These are often the skills most readily acquired through employment-based training - learning experiences graduates have limited access to.

## Growth in the incidence of training

**4.51** Much of the growth in qualifications documented above has arisen from the expansion in formal education. However, there are large numbers of people with either low level or no vocational qualifications already in the labour market who are unlikely to be able to raise their qualification levels through formal education. Skills can also be developed through workplace learning which has a vital role to play if the UK is to develop a world class workforce. Indeed it may constitute the only way of upgrading the skills and qualifications of many adults who have become disillusioned with formal education.

**4.52** Much of the training that takes place in the workplace is relatively informal (Stern et al. 1999). This includes learning by doing and learning by example. Intuitively one might expect many low qualified individuals to be more comfortable learning in this way than in more formal settings which bear closer resemblance to the classroom-based courses where they enjoyed limited success in the past. Informal learning is not readily measured by formal statistical surveys. Generally respondents tend to adopt a relatively narrow definition of training (Felstead et al. 1997) and as a result recorded statistics may underestimate the extent of training activity.

**4.53** The great majority - 90% - of workplaces in Britain offer some form of training to some of their employees. Evidence from IALS indicates that 39 per cent of employees received training in the 12 months before the survey. There is evidence from LFS and IALS that measured training levels have increased over the last fifteen years although over the last five years the picture seems to be fairly static. For example, the proportion of the workforce receiving any job-related training during the last month rose by nearly 5 percentage points between 1985 and 1994, but has risen by only 1.8 percentage points between 1995 and 1999 to stand at 15 per cent in autumn 1999 (LFS).

**4.54** Some research has suggested that the growing incidence of training in the 1980s may be due to increased requirements from health and safety and product quality regulations at the time, including British Standard 5750 (Felstead and Green, 1996). This research suggests that the rise in participation in training has been balanced by a fall in the length of training (Green 1999). Other research suggests that the growth in short duration training is due to the changing structure of the workforce towards workers more likely to experience short duration training events (e.g. part-time workers) than factors related to a growing demand for health and safety and quality standards training (Arulampalam et al, 1998).

**4.55** Against the rise in the incidence of training about one third of employees report never having been offered any kind of training by their current employers during the last year. Generally, those that do not receive training in a given year are less likely to receive training over even longer time periods.

## Training provision skewed to the most able

**4.56** The distribution of training varies greatly by occupation and mode of employment. In general the highest levels of training are received by highly-qualified people. The LFS shows that 20% of those qualified at Level 4 or above (sub-degree, degree and post-graduate level qualifications) received training funded by their employer in the four weeks prior to the survey. This compares to 12% of those with qualifications at 'GCSE' and 'A' level (and equivalent), and 7% or less of those qualified below Level 2 (Figure 4.5). As we would expect this uneven distribution carries over when looking at the incidence of training by occupation. For example, LFS data show that over 40% of employees in professional or associate professional occupations had received training over a recent thirteen-week period compared to under 20 per cent of craft employees and less than one in seven of operatives (see Table 4.6).

**4.57** The evidence is clear that well-qualified individuals are far more likely to receive training and acquire more skills in later life than their less qualified counterparts. This unequal distribution of training seems to compound the inequality between those with and those without intermediate to higher level qualifications. Therefore current levels of training are unlikely to either:

* raise the qualification levels of the significant number of adults with no or low level qualifications, or

* improve the shortfall of vocational qualifications at Levels 2 and 3 in the UK relative to some of its main competitors.

**Figure 4.5: Employees receiving job-related training by highest qualification**

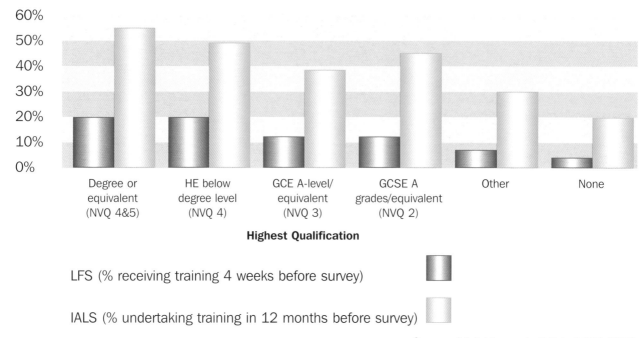

**Highest Qualification**

LFS (% receiving training 4 weeks before survey)

IALS (% undertaking training in 12 months before survey)

Source: Adult Literacy in Britain 1997 (IALS)

## Part-time and temporary workers

**4.58** More flexible ways of working are becoming more common with increasing numbers of part-time and temporary workers. Table 4.6 suggests that such workers are less likely to receive training. For example, IALS finds that full-time workers are roughly twice as likely to have received training during the previous twelve months compared with part-time workers. Arulampalam et al (1998) similarly found that those in part-time employment and those on fixed-term contracts were less likely to receive training.

**4.59** However, the evidence on training received by part-time and temporary workers is inconclusive. Green (1999) finds that the incidence of training amongst part-time workers is comparable with those working full-time whilst the incidence of training is actually higher amongst those on fixed-term employees compared with those on permanent contracts. The latter is partly due to the greater incidence of induction training amongst fixed-term employees.

**Table 4.6: Employees receiving job-related training, by occupation and terms of employment**

| | Measure of employer provided training: | |
| --- | --- | --- |
| | **LFS** (percentage receiving training in the 13 weeks before survey) | **IALS** (percentage undertaking training in the 12 months before survey) |
| **All employees** | 28.0 % | 39 % |
| **Occupation** | | |
| Managers and administrators | 31.2 % | 45 % |
| Professional | 46.4 % | 56 % |
| Associate professional, technical | 44.6 % | 56 % |
| Clerical and secretarial | 26.6 % | 42 % |
| Craft and related | 19.8 % | 28 % |
| Personal and protective services | 29.4 % | 34 % |
| Sales | 24.1 % | 35 % |
| Plant and machine operatives | 13.5 % | 30 % |
| Other | 12.3 % | 19 % |
| **Employment status** | | |
| Permanent employee | 28.0 % | n/a |
| Temporary employee | 30.4 % | n/a |
| **Hours of work** | | |
| Full-time | 29.5 % | 46 % |
| Part-time | 23.4 % | 28 % |

Source: LFS, Spring 1998; IALS

### Small firms least likely to train

**4.60** One of the main differences in the provision of training by different types of firm is that smaller firms, and particularly the very smallest, are much less likely to provide training. SNIB shows that 79% of firms with 25-49 employees provide some off-the-job training compared with 92% of firms who employ 200 or more. However, the difference is particularly notable when a comparison is made with the SNIB survey of firms with fewer than 25 employees, only 36% of which provided some off-the-job training for their employees.

**4.61** These differences partly reflect the fact that smaller firms tend to incur higher unit training costs. For example, they face disproportionate costs for covering for absent staff, they are less likely to have any internal training capacity and they are unlikely to enjoy economies of scale from purchasing training in bulk. A recent BCC survey found that only 1 in 5 companies with fewer than 50 staff have internal personnel or training staff of any kind (BCC, 1999). The lack of internal career paths in smaller firms often makes small firms less willing to train workers who might be poached by competing firms before they can recoup their training costs.

**4.62** Formal surveys may underestimate the extent to which small firms train and develop their workers since informal learning tends to go unreported. Such training may take place during the course of a normal working day and so can avoid the need to cover for absent staff. It is also directly linked to workers' productivity in their current job and can generate immediate benefits. Whether or not small firms are more likely to exploit these potential benefits of informal training is debatable. Generally the incidence of informal learning appears to be positively associated with the motivation and enthusiasm of managers at all levels and the introduction of new work practices.

## Much training is short term

**4.63** In addition to concerns about the distribution and quantity of training activity, the other major area of potential concern is the quality of training received. Unfortunately this aspect is particularly difficult to measure and at best we have to rely on proxies. The most common proxies are i) whether or not training leads to a qualification and ii) how long it lasts.

**4.64** In terms of qualifications, the LFS shows that 39% of employer-funded training leads to either a qualification or a credit towards a qualification. This is similar to the figure in IALS where 41% of taught-learning episodes were designed to lead to a full or part qualification. The LFS shows that in the majority of cases the qualifications being aimed for are relatively high level ones, with 70% being accounted for by degree level qualifications or "other professional" qualifications. Six percent are nursing qualifications and only 12% are accounted for by a combination of intermediate level vocational qualifications including NVQs, City and Guilds, RSA and BTEC. This implies that those who are already more highly skilled and more highly qualified are most likely to benefit from training which is transferable and certified - and, as noted above, they are more likely to receive training in the first place. This evidence again suggests that the gap between the more and the less qualified is accentuated by current training activity. It also implies that current training volumes will not raise intermediate vocational skills in the UK to levels which are comparable with those in leading competitor countries.

**4.65** As far as the duration of training is concerned, a substantial proportion covers only short periods. Forty four percent of employer-funded training recorded in the LFS lasts for less than one week. On the other hand, 17% of it lasts for between 6 months and 3 years with a further 28% lasting for over 3 years or described as ongoing. There is likely to be some overlap between this latter category and the elements of training which are leading to degree level and professional qualifications. IALS found that most training received was at a very low level and often it is of relatively short duration. EMPSS data shows that only 4% of employers had provided 10 or more days training per head on average (Dench, 1993a, 1993b).

# The future supply of qualifications

**4.66** Much of the projected rise in qualifications is expected to occur at higher levels. This reflects the likely continued attractiveness of acquiring these levels of qualification in terms of returns in the labour market and the continued expansion of Higher Education places. IER project the flow (i.e. new labour market entrants) of Higher Education qualifiers between 1997/98 to 2009 to be about 3 million. Combined with expected activity rates, this is expected to raise the stock of the labour force qualified to at least NVQ Level 4 by 2.1 million between 1998 and 2009 so that by then 30% of those in employment are qualified to this level.

**4.67** Most of this increase in the stock will be amongst those acquiring first degrees or their equivalents (1.6 million) but there is also expected to be a considerable increase in the stock of post-graduates in the labour market (460,000).

**4.68** Rapid growth at degree level is expected to compensate for substantially lower growth at NVQ Level 4 other than degree level.[12] The supply of people with NVQ 4 vocational qualifications other than degrees is expected to grow at a much more modest 10% between now and 2009. The number of those employed with HNC and other Level 4 vocational qualifications is expected to increase by around 70 thousand (just over 5%) while the stock of those with nursing and teaching qualifications at this level is expected to rise by over 100 thousand (3%).

**4.69** Forecasting the supply of lower level qualifications is more difficult. This is partly because historical data are not available for many of these other qualifications. The available data on stocks concentrates on highest qualification held while that on flows fails to distinguish prior qualifications held. This means that it has been impossible to project trends for these qualification levels.

# Summary

**4.70** There are few statistical surveys which aim to produce direct measures of the skill level of the workforce. The review of skills supply in this chapter reflects this and uses qualifications as a proxy indicator of skill whilst recognising the limitations of this approach.

**4.71** For several decades participation in post-compulsory education has been increasing. This has led to rising attainment amongst new labour market entrants. Levels of attainment have risen in all parts of the formal education system. A-levels remain the most popular form of study for 16-18 year olds although the vast majority of young people do not study or pass A-level mathematics. This has had implications for the numbers eligible to enter technical and high value-added degree courses such as engineering.

**4.72** The introduction of NVQs and GNVQs contributed to a substantial growth in the number of young people gaining vocational qualifications although most of these have been concentrated at low levels (below Level 3) and in relatively few disciplines. Consequently, the UK remains a long way behind some of its international competitors in terms of the proportion of young people entering the labour market with intermediate vocational qualifications, particularly at Level 3.

---

[12] These projections did not attempt to estimate the impact of the new Associate Degree.

**4.73** During the late 1980s and early 1990s there was a very large expansion in Higher Education. Most of this expansion has taken place at degree level and above. Although Higher Education is traditionally regarded as academic or general education, a large part of the expansion has occurred in relatively new vocationally orientated courses such as computing, design and business studies. In contrast, the growth in some of the more traditional Higher Education degree courses has been slower and some, like general engineering and chemistry, have started to decline.

**4.74** To some extent, trends in Higher Education may compensate for the relatively smaller numbers achieving vocational qualifications at Level 3 and above. This is reflected in the growing number of graduates entering associate professional and technical level jobs. There is evidence that graduates entering these jobs may not possess the range of work experience, business awareness and generic skills employers are looking for.

**4.75** The rise in attainment amongst young people has contributed to substantial growth in the qualifications held by the UK workforce. However, in spite of this:

- over one-half of the UK workforce still have either low or no qualifications;

- the UK still falls a long way short of some of its main competitors in terms of the proportion of the labour force holding vocational qualifications at Levels two and three;

- around one fifth of adults have poor basic skills.

**4.76** Therefore, whilst the education system is helping to raise attainment amongst more, predominantly young people, a substantial proportion of adults still have relatively low qualifications. Work based learning provides a means of raising skills and qualifications amongst all adults including those who leave formal education with no qualifications. Indeed, learning at work may be more effective for those with lower qualifications. However, the low qualified receive relatively little training. Consequently, current measurable training activity appears unlikely to raise the qualification levels of those with low or no qualifications or raise the proportion of people with good basic skills.

**4.77** The evidence reviewed in this chapter has shown that skills as measured by qualifications have risen substantially during the last twenty years. However, most growth at higher levels has occurred in Higher Education whilst vocational attainment remains at relatively low levels. The majority do not gain intermediate competence in mathematics despite the relatively high returns to such qualifications and there are still many people with no qualifications and a significant proportion with poor basic skills. Neither current trends in education nor workplace learning appear set to change these trends. Consequently, it is expected that much of the growth in qualifications during the next decade will continue to be concentrated in Higher Education. Attainment in vocational qualifications is likely to remain at relatively low levels and significantly behind some of our main European partners should current trends persist. There is little evidence that the 'long tail' of low achievement will be corrected as those who do not achieve qualifications at school and those with poor basic skills are less likely to take part in education or training in later life.

# Annex 1

## Allocating qualifications to NVQ level (UK)

The following tables relate to Figure 4.1 and Table 4.1 and show what qualifications were allocated to each of the NVQ Levels for 1997 onwards, 1989 and 1979

### Labour Force Survey Spring 1997 onwards

| Qualification | Degree and above | L4 below degree | Level 3 | Level 2 | Level 1 |
|---|---|---|---|---|---|
| Higher degree | ✓ | | | | |
| NVQ Level 5 | ✓ | | | | |
| First degree | ✓ | | | | |
| Other degree | ✓ | | | | |
| NVQ Level 4 | ✓ | | | | |
| Teaching, further education | ✓ | | | | |
| Teaching, secondary education | ✓ | | | | |
| Teaching, primary education | ✓ | | | | |
| Teaching, level not stated | ✓ | | | | |
| Nursing etc | ✓ | | | | |
| Diploma in higher education | | General | | | |
| Other HE below degree | | General | | | |
| HNC, HND, BTEC etc higher | | Vocational | | | |
| RSA higher diploma | | Vocational | | | |
| A-level or equivalent | | | General (73%) - those with 2+ | General (27%) those with 1 | |
| Scottish CSYS | | | General (67%) | General L2 (33%) | |
| SCE higher or equivalent | | | General (58%) - those with 3+ | General (42%) - those with 1 or 2 | |
| A,S level or equivalent | | | General (0%) - those with 4+ | General (15%) - those with 2 or 3 | General (85%) - those with 1 |
| RSA advanced diploma | | | Vocational | | |
| OND, ONC, BTEC etc, national | | | Vocational | | |
| City & Guilds advanced craft | | | Vocational | | |
| Trade apprenticeship | | | Vocational (50%) | Vocational (50%) | |
| NVQ Level 3 | | | Vocational | | |
| GNVQ advanced | | | Vocational | | |
| O level, GCSE grade A-C or equivalent | | | | General (49%) - those with 5+ | General (51%) - those with <5 |
| NVQ Level 2 | | | | Vocational | |
| GNVQ intermediate | | | | Vocational | |
| RSA diploma | | | | Vocational | |
| City & Guilds craft | | | | Vocational | |

Continued

Continued

| | | | | | |
|---|---|---|---|---|---|
| BTEC,SCOTVEC first or general diploma | | | Vocational | | |
| CSE below grade1, GCSE below grade C | | | | | General |
| NVQ Level 1 | | | | | Vocational |
| GNVQ, GSVQ foundation level | | | | | Vocational |
| BTEC, SCOTVEC first or general certificate | | | Vocational | | |
| SCOTVEC modules | | | | | Vocational |
| RSA other | | | | | Vocational |
| City & Guilds other | | | | | Vocational |
| YT,YTP certificate | | | | | Vocational |
| Other Qualifications | | | Other qualifications (10%) | Other qualifications (35%) | Other qualifications (55%) |
| Don't know/NA | pro rata | pro rata | pro rata | pro rata | pro rata |

## Labour Force Survey 1989

| Qualification | Degree and above | L4 below degree | Level 3 | Level 2 | Level 1 |
|---|---|---|---|---|---|
| Degree or equivalent: | ✓ | | | | |
| Higher | ✓ | | | | |
| First | ✓ | | | | |
| Other | ✓ | | | | |
| Teaching, further education | ✓ | | | | |
| Teaching, secondary | ✓ | | | | |
| Teaching, primary | ✓ | | | | |
| Nursing | ✓ | | | | |
| BTEC/SCOTBTEC/HND etc | | Vocational | | | |
| A-level | | | General (70%) | General (30%) | |
| BTEC/SCOTBTEC/OND etc | | | Vocational (70%) | Vocational (15%) | Vocational (15%) |
| City & Guilds | | | Vocational (20%) | Vocational (40%) | Vocational (40%) |
| Trade apprenticeship | | | Vocational (50%) | Vocational (50%) | |
| O level/CSE grade 1 etc | | | | General (60%) | General (40%) |
| CSE (other grades) | | | | | General |
| YTS certificate | | | | | Vocational |
| Other qualifications | | | Other qualifications (10%) | Other qualifications (35%) | Other qualifications (55%) |
| Don't know/NA | pro rata | | pro rata | pro rata | pro rata |

## Labour Force Survey 1979

| Qualification | Degree and above | L4 below degree | Level 3 | Level 2 | Level 1 |
|---|---|---|---|---|---|
| First or higher degree | ✓ | | | | |
| Corp or grad. member of prof. inst. | ✓ | | | | |
| Secondary | ✓ | | | | |
| Primary | ✓ | | | | |
| Nursing qualification | ✓ | | | | |
| HNC/HND | | Vocational | | | |
| A-level or equivalent | | | General (70%) | General (30%) | |
| ONC/OND | | | Vocational (70%) | Vocational (15%) | Vocational (15%) |
| City and Guilds | | | Vocational (20%) | Vocational (40%) | Vocational (40%) |
| Trade apprenticeship completed | | | Vocational (50%) | Vocational (50%) | |
| O level or equivalent | | | | General (60%) | General (40%) |
| CSE (other grades) | | | | | General |
| Any other professional vocational qualification | | | Vocational (10%) | Vocational (35%) | Vocational (55%) |
| Still studying/Not known/ No reply/Not applicable | pro rata | | pro rata | pro rata | pro rata |

## Footnotes to Annex 2 pages 82 & 83

[13] This was allocated to <Level 2 because all apprenticeship certificates in the other countries examined were only awarded to candidates who also passed written technical and general examinations.

[14] In order to create a consistent time-series from 1985 onwards we were obliged to put all City & Guilds certificates into a single category. These include single subject certificates, Part 1, Part 2 and Part 3 awards. The estimate of 40% represents the share taken by single subject certificates and Part 1 awards.

[15] This figure is slightly less than the percentage gaining 5 Grade A-C passes at GCSE. In fact it is chosen as a proxy for the percentage of O-level holders who have passes at Grades A-C in Mathematics, English and one other subject. This grouping was chosen since all the comparator qualifications in other countries were grouped certificates which required a pass in Mathematics, the language of instruction and at least one other subject for the award. However, it could be argued that this figure is rather generous especially with respect to the younger age groups. The figure of 40% is, of course, based on flows of individuals before they proceed to other qualifications. It seems likely that most of those who have obtained Maths, English and one other subject at GCSE grades A-C will obtain a higher qualification. Those left may well be predominantly less qualified. However, the allocation of only 30% of the adult population with O-level to Level 2 is probably an under-estimate of those in this group.

[16] This proxies those who do not obtain at least two A-levels i.e. university entrance level qualification. All qualifications at this level in France and Germany confer the right to proceed to university and test a range of subjects.

[17] This is a grouped examination consisting of 3 externally set and marked written papers in French, mathematics and history/geography together with teacher assessment in other subjects. Some 11% of all those who pass take a special series designed for those who study in a vocational college. We consider these to be below the standard of the main examination and have therefore assigned it to this level.

[18] These are rigorous vocational examinations which require a pass in written general examinations and practical tests. The BEP requires three years of study post Brevet and it is difficult to decide whether to classify it as equivalent to, at least, an NVQ 3 pass. However, the French authorities do not recognise the BEP as a Level 3 qualification since it does not give access to university. We have therefore assigned it to Level 2.

[19] This category is highly problematic. The change in the composition of this category after 1991 and the reasons for the change can be found at http://cep.lse.ac.uk/datalib/training/germany/mikrozensus.htm

[20] Apprenticeships where the holders have a school leaving certificate from the Hauptschule or the Realschule have been discounted to allow for the small proportion of apprenticeships which are of two rather than 3 or 3+ years duration.

# Annex 2

## Allocating qualifications to NVQ level (international comparisons)

The following information relates to the Steedman (1999) data quoted in this chapter and presented in table 4.2. It presents what qualifications for each country were allocated to each NVQ qualification level.

**UNITED KINGDOM**

### < Level 2

- Don't Know 100%
- No qualifications 100%
- Other vocational qualifications 55%
- CSE < Grade 1 100%
- One or more O-level passes 60% (Active population and 16-64 year-olds 70%)
- Apprenticeship without recognised vocational qualification 100%[13]
- City & Guilds qualification 40%[14]

### Level 2

- Other vocational qualifications 35%
- One or more O-level passes 40% (Active population and 16-64 year-olds 30%)[15]
- (G) NVQ 2 (from 1996 onwards)
- One or more A-level 20 % (Active population and 16-64 year-olds 30%)[16]
- City & Guilds qualification 40%

### Level 3

- Other vocational qualifications 10%
- (G) NVQ 3 (from 1996)
- One or more A-level 80% (Active population and 16-64 year-olds 70%)
- City & Guilds 20%
- BTEC ONC/OND 100%

### > Level 3

- Nursing 100%
- Primary Teaching 100%
- Secondary Teaching 100%
- BTEC HNC/HND 100%
- Other degree 100%
- First degree 100%
- Higher degree 100%

**FRANCE**

**< Level 2**

- Don't Know 100%
- No qualification or only Certificate of Primary Education 100%
- Brevet 11%[17]

**Level 2**

- Brevet 89%
- CAP/BEP 100%[18]

**Level 3**

- Baccalaureat (General, Technical and Vocational) or Vocational Brevet 100%

**> Level 3**

- Qualifications requiring two years of study after the Baccalaureat 100%
- All degrees and higher degrees 100%

**GERMANY**

**Level 1**

- Others ( includes Don't Know, No Response and No Qualifications)100%[19]
- Leaving Certificate of the Secondary Modern School (Hauptschulabschluss) 100%

**Level 2**

- Leaving School Certificate of the *Realschule* 100%
- Apprenticeship without prior school leaving qualification 100%
- Apprenticeship with prior school leaving qualification 6% (Active population and 16-64 10%)[20]

**Level 3**

- Apprenticeship with prior school leaving qualification 94% (Active population and 16-64 90%)
- *Hochschulreife* (Qualification giving right to enter university or *Fachhochschule*)100%
- *Fachhochschulreife* (Qualification giving right to enter *Fachhochschule*)100%

**>Level 3**

- *Meister* or *Techniker* certificate or *Fachschulabschluss* 100%
- Degree qualification from *Fachhochschule* 100%
- Degree or higher degree from University 100%

## REFERENCES

Arulampalam, W., Booth, A.L. and Elias, P. (1998) *The Incidence and duration of work-related training in the UK* TSER STT Working paper.

British Chambers of Commerce (BCC) (1999) "Parental Leave Survey", July 1999.

Carey, S. Low, S. and Hansbro, J. (1997) "Adult Literacy in Britain" ONS The Stationary Office.

Dench, S. (1993a). "Employers' Provision of Continual Training". *Social Science Research Branch Working Paper* No.6, London: Employment Department (mimeo).

Dench, S. (1993b). "Why do Employers Train?", *Social Science Research Branch Working Paper* No.5, London: Employment Department (mimeo).

DfEE (2000) "Vocational Qualifications in the UK: 1998/9" *Statistical Bulletin* (forthcoming).

DfEE/Cabinet Office (1996), *Competitiveness Occasional Paper. The Skills Audit: A Report from an Interdepartmental Group.*

European Commission (1998), *Education across the European Union* - statistics and indicators, 1998.

Green, F. (1999) "Training The Workers", in *The State of Working Britain"*. Ed by P. Gregg and L. Wadsworth. Manchester, Manchester University Press: 127-146.

Hansen, K and Vignoles, A. (1999) *International Comparisons of HE Entrance Requirements for Computer Science and Engineering Graduates: UK.* Unpublished report for DfEE.

Felstead, A., Green, F. and Mayhew, K. (1997) "Getting the Measure of Training. A Report on Training Statistics in Britain" Centre for Industrial Policy and Performance University of Leeds.

Felstead, A. and Green, F. (1996) "Training implications of regulation compliance and business cycles" in A.L. Booth and D.J. Snower (eds) *Acquiring Skills. Market Failures, their symptoms and policy responses.* Cambridge, Cambridge University Press.

Institute for Employment Studies 1993 "Basic Skills and Jobs" ALBSU.

Mason, G. (2000) "The Mix of Graduate and Intermediate-level Skills in Britain: What Should the Balance Be?" *Journal of Education and Work* (forthcoming).

Mason, G. (1999) "The Labour Market for Engineering, Science and IT Graduates: Are there mismatches between supply and demand?" Research Report 112, Department for Education and Employment.

Steedman, H., Vignoles, A., Bruniaux, C., Wagner, K., and Hansen, K. (2000) "International Comparisons of HE Quality: Engineering and Computer Science" Unpublished report to DfEE.

Steedman, H. (1999) "Report to the Department of Education and Employment: Updatng of Skills Audit Data 1998" Provisional interim report. Centre for Economic Performance. LSE.

Stern, E. and E. Sommerlad (1999). *Workplace Learning, Culture and Performance* (Issues in People Management Series), London: Institute of Personnel and Development.

Vignoles, A and Hansen, K (2000) *Relative Wages of Computer Scientists and Engineers in the UK Graduate Labour Market.* Draft Report to DfEE.

Wilson, R, A. (2000) "Projections of Occupations and Qualifications" IER.

# CHAPTER 5
## THE BALANCE BETWEEN SKILLS SUPPLY AND DEMAND: SKILL-RELATED RECRUITMENT DIFFICULTIES

## Introduction

**5.1**  Chapter 3 presented evidence of rising demand for a wide range of generic and vocational skills in many industries and occupations.  Chapter 4 analysed recent trends in the supply of skills and concluded that - in spite of recent growth in participation in full-time education and in workplace training - the British economy continues to suffer from certain weaknesses in skills acquisition, in particular, at basic and intermediate skill levels and in some areas of high-level technical skills and knowledge.  The next step is to go on to consider available evidence on the extent and nature of *imbalances between skills supply and demand* as reported by employers (Chapters 5 and 6) and as manifested in recent changes in market salaries and the financial returns to the acquisition of different types of qualification (Chapter 7).

**5.2**  The evidence presented below draws heavily on the results of new research which was commissioned by the Skills Task Force during 1999.  In a large-scale investigation, the Task Force commissioned a telephone survey of just over 23000 employers and a face-to-face survey of nearly 4000 employers which, taken together, constitute a nationally representative sample of all establishments in England with 5 or more employees.[1]  In addition, intensive case study investigations were carried out in 95 workplaces in seven different industries (banking and finance, telecommunications, hotels, food processing, engineering, health and social care, local and central government).  This new evidence has contributed to the comprehensive review of the incidence, scale and commercial impact of different kinds of skill problems experienced by employers presented in this and the following chapter.

**5.3**  This chapter is particularly concerned with the extent and nature of skill-related recruitment difficulties as perceived by employers.  In the next section the term 'skill shortages' is defined. It looks at the extent of employers' recruitment problems and whether they are related to skills issues.  It also looks at the skills which are most affected and the potential impacts on business performance of skill-related recruitment difficulties.  The final section of this chapter summarises the evidence presented and conclusions drawn.

---

[1]  All business sectors (public and private) were covered, with the exception of Agriculture, Hunting and Forestry (1992 SIC codes 01-02), Fishing (1992 SIC codes 05) and Private Households with Employed Persons (1992 SIC codes 95).

## 'Skill Shortages': Definitional issues

**5.4** Analysis of 'skill shortages' is frequently hampered by inconsistencies in definition and measurement. In a survey of skill shortage studies during the 1970s and 1980s, Meager (1986) identified two very different approaches which are commonly adopted in order to address the main issues of interest:

- an 'employer perspective' which defines shortages in terms of recruitment difficulties experienced by individual employers (even if the causes of difficulty are purely internal to the firm, e.g. unwillingness to pay competitive salaries); and

- a 'market perspective' which recognises shortages only if there are insufficient 'appropriate people in the market, to fill existing posts at going wages'.

**5.5** However, even within these two different perspectives, there is evidence of inconsistency in the way that terms are used. For example, Green and Ashton (1992) note that skill shortages taking the form of external recruitment difficulties are frequently conflated with internal skill deficiencies, that is, gaps between firms' current skill levels and some desired or optimum level of skills. Similarly, market-based definitions of shortages date back to early studies which expected 'true' shortages to manifest themselves - eventually, if not immediately - in upward adjustments of relative salary levels for the skill or occupation in question (Blank and Stigler, 1957; Arrow and Capron, 1959). However, it was quickly recognised that salary adjustments of this kind could be impeded by various factors such as delays by employers in accepting the needs for such increases and a reluctance to disturb existing salary structures in order to raise salaries for new employees with the required skills (Arrow and Capron, 1959).

**5.6** Other problems in the analysis of skill shortages are raised by Hart (1990) who distinguishes between *ex ante* (anticipated) skill shortages - which employers may seek to counteract in a variety of ways - and *ex post* (actual) skill shortages which may have adverse effects on company output and performance. Employers typically develop a range of responses and 'coping mechanisms' in an effort to minimise the impact of anticipated shortages, for example, working more overtime, increasing subcontracting, recruiting staff at a lower level than previously hoped for or retraining existing staff. Hence, actual shortages are very often smaller in scale than those which were initially anticipated. However, the measures taken to reduce their impact typically impose additional costs on employers and may well restrict their ability to achieve desired quality standards.

**5.7** Taking account of these issues and building on the vocabulary the Task Force used in its first report, this chapter and the next focus on two very different kinds of skill deficiency or problem with which employers may be confronted:

**i.** *external skill shortages,* that is, recruitment difficulties due to an excess of demand over supply of required skills in the external labour market (this chapter)

**ii.** *internal skill gaps,* that is, a divergence between firms' current skill levels and those which are required to meet firms' business objectives (Chapter 6)

# External skill shortages

## Trends over time in recruitment difficulties

**5.8** Surveys of recruitment difficulties (or hard-to-fill vacancies) have over many years consistently pointed to the following main conclusions:

- The reported incidence of such problems is heavily cyclical in nature.

- Not all hard-to-fill vacancies are the product of excess demand for skills in the labour market. A large proportion of such vacancies are attributable to company-specific factors such as limited efforts at job advertising or the relatively unattractive salaries or job conditions on offer.

- In many cases the difficulties in filling vacancies derive from perceived shortcomings in the 'quality' of job applicants even though there may be little or no deficiency in quantitative terms.

**5.9** The longest data series available on employers' experience of skill problems comes from the CBI's quarterly Industrial Trends Survey which asks manufacturing employers[2] to indicate whether skilled labour is likely to limit their output in the following four-month period. This question lends itself to different interpretations and a recent follow-up study of survey participants suggested that about 60% of respondents interpreted the question as referring to external recruitment difficulties while 45% thought it referred to the skills possessed by their existing workforce (Mann and Junankar, 1998).

**5.10** As Figure 5.1 shows, the reported incidence of skilled labour constraints has risen rapidly during periods of rapid economic growth and falling unemployment while reaching its lowest levels during peak periods of unemployment such as in the early 1980s and early 1990s. In the current business cycle, the proportion of manufacturing employers citing such constraints peaked at 15% in late 1998 although unemployment has continued to fall since that time.[3]

**5.11** The most recent CBI data are broadly consistent with the last Skill Needs in Britain (SNIB) survey which was carried out in May-June 1998 and was based on a nationally representative sample of 4000 establishments employing 25 or more people. It found that some 19% of manufacturing employers were experiencing hard-to-fill vacancies at the time of interview, compared to 23-25% in service sectors. Across the whole economy the proportions of establishments reporting hard-to-fill vacancies ranged from 20% in the 25-49 employee size-group to 33% in the 500-plus size-group (IFF, 1998).

**5.12** The most commonly cited occupations with hard-to-fill vacancies fall into two distinct categories. On the one hand, there are some relatively low paid occupations with traditionally high rates of turnover which may be regarded as perennially hard to fill (for example, catering occupations, counter hands and hospital porters). On the other hand, recruitment difficulties were also reported during 1998 for more highly-paid occupations requiring specific technical qualifications such as engineers and technologists and health and related occupations (IFF, 1998) and craft and technician vacancies in the engineering industry (EMTA/EEF, 1999).

---

[2] The CBI survey also covers mining and printing & publishing; however, the overwhelming majority of survey respondents are engaged in different kinds of manufacturing.

[3] This 1998 peak is some way below earlier peaks in 1988-89 (25%) and 1978-79 (23%). Detailed analysis of CBI survey data by Blake et al (2000) suggests that this trend decline in reported skill problems may owe more to the decline in manufacturing output and employment over the period than to any improvement in the workings of the labour market. Indeed, there is statistical evidence that periodic increases in the proportion of employers reporting skill problems since the 1960s may have actually contributed to subsequent falls in output and employment.

**Figure 5.1: Skilled labour constraints on output in manufacturing companies and unemployed as a percent of total workforce, 1967-99 (four-quarter moving averages of quarterly data)**

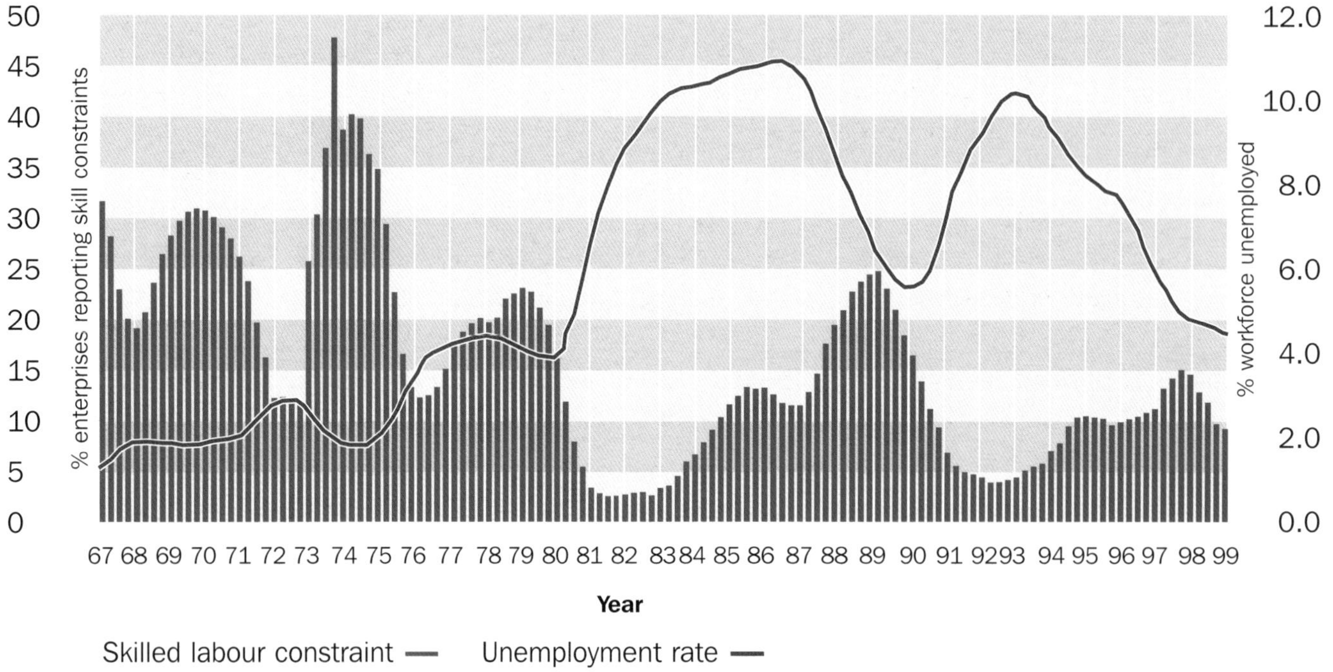

Skilled labour constraint —     Unemployment rate —

Source: CBI Industrial Trends Survey; NIESR estimates

Notes: (a) Skilled labour constraint series shows proportion of CBI survey respondents who answered 'yes' to the question: 'Is shortage of skilled labour likely to limit your output over the next 4 months?' (b) Unemployment rate defined as claimant unemployed as percent of total (employed plus unemployed).

**5.13** In some cases, recurrent excesses of demand over supply for certain skilled and/or highly qualified positions may reflect the long duration of the training required to achieve the desired skill levels and the delayed impact which occurs when training is cut back during periods of recession. This contributes to later shortages of such skills when the economy recovers, for example, apprentice-trained craftspeople in engineering (Mason, 1999). In other cases, the shortfall in supply may be attributed to the relatively weak salary and other incentives for young people to make the study and career choices which are necessary for certain positions to be filled, for example, secondary school teachers in subjects such as maths and physics. However, hard-to-fill vacancies also arise from time to time due to exceptionally rapid growth and rapid change in some sectors of the economy which result in excess demand for certain scarce and highly-valued skills, for example, knowledge and experience of recently developed computer languages and systems (IT NTO, 1999).

**5.14** Other explanations for recurring difficulties in filling certain positions derive from apparent problems in the 'quality' of job applicants, even though there appears to be little or no shortfall in quantity. For example, some employers complain about shortcomings in the basic literacy and numeracy of poorly educated job seekers. At the other end of the education scale, there has been a steady flow of reports in recent years which emphasise the perceived weaknesses of many new graduates in communication and inter personal skills, commercial understanding and sometimes in technical skills and knowledge as well (IRS, 1995; IPD, 1997; AGR, 1997, 1998).

## Recent evidence on recruitment difficulties

**5.15** Consider the results from the Skills Survey (ESS) of just under 27,000 establishments which was carried out between August and November 1999.[4] Its findings suggest that, at any given point in time during this period, there were approximately 560,000 job vacancies in England (in establishments with five or more employees). This is equivalent to around 3% of employment and is roughly 2.3 times the total number of unfilled vacancies reported to the Employment Service (ES) in July 1999. As shown in Table 5.1, the occupational distribution of vacancies in the surveyed establishments differed sharply from ES vacancies with smaller proportions of unfilled positions in personal service and other manual occupations and larger proportions of associate professional, professional, managerial and sales positions.

**Table 5.1: Unfilled vacancies reported to Employment Service and estimated total vacancies, hard-to-fill vacancies and external skill shortages in England, analysed by occupational category**

| | Employment Service England, July 1999 Unfilled vacancies | SURVEY-BASED ESTIMATES: | | |
| --- | --- | --- | --- | --- |
| | | Total unfilled vacancies | Total hard-to-fill vacancies | Total external skill shortages (b) |
| **Total no. of vacancies** | **248828** | **560000** | **255000** | **110000** |
| | Percentages | | | |
| Managers/senior administrators | 4 | 7 | 5 | 7 |
| Professional | 1 | 6 | 5 | 8 |
| Associate professional/ technical | 3 | 11 | 12 | 17 |
| Clerical/secretarial | 14 | 16 | 9 | 9 |
| Craft and skilled | 10 | 8 | 14 | 22 |
| Personal service | 24 | 15 | 17 | 11 |
| Sales | 14 | 19 | 16 | 13 |
| Operative and assembly | 10 | 11 | 13 | 9 |
| Other manual occupations | 18 | 7 | 7 | 3 |
| **Total** | **100** | **100** | **100** | **100** |

Note: (a) Survey-based estimates refer to establishments with five or more employees. (b) Refers to skill-related hard-to-fill vacancies defined as those for which at least one of the following causes of hard-to-fill vacancies was cited: 'Low number of applicants with the required skills'; 'Lack of work experience the company demands'; 'Lack of qualifications the company demands'.

[4] See Paragraph 5.2 for details.

## Figure 5.2: Total external skill shortages by occupation

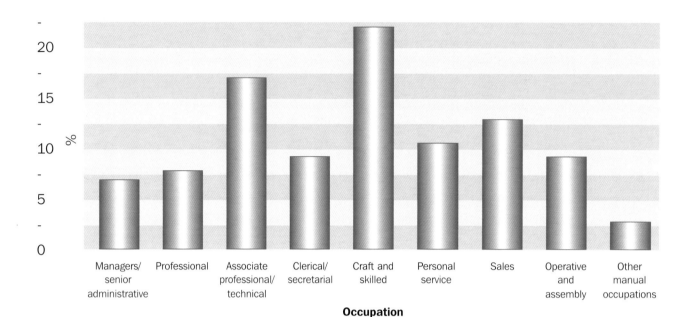

**5.16** Many of these vacancies are of short duration and reflect the natural functioning of the labour market. The concern here is hard-to-fill vacancies and particularly those related to genuine shortages of skill. In the ESS an estimated 255,000 (46%) of unfilled vacancies were described as hard-to-fill and of these some 110,000 positions were 'skill-related' in that that they were explicitly attributed to a lack of job applicants with the required skills, qualifications or work experience.[5] These skill-related hard-to-fill vacancies will be defined here as 'external skill shortages'.

**5.17** About one in twelve establishments in the survey reported having at least one external skill shortage (roughly half of all establishments with hard-to-fill vacancies of some kind). Although the overall proportion of establishments reporting external skill shortages is relatively small, it represents one in four of all establishments who were actually seeking to fill vacancies at the time of the survey, including many of the fastest-growing and most dynamic establishments.[6] In general, the incidence of external skill shortages was substantially greater in large establishments than in small and medium-sized ones and was also greater in southern and eastern regions than in the Midlands or North of England.

**5.18** About four in every ten external skill shortages were in craft and technical occupations. The extent of problems in these areas is even more apparent when one considers that these two occupations account for less than 1 in 4 of all jobs. However, not all external skill shortages were associated with what are normally considered to be skilled jobs. Around one-quarter of these types of vacancy were found in personal service and sales occupations. As with craft and technical occupations, the proportions of hard-to-fill vacancies in these occupations were much higher than their shares of total employment (only 1 in 7 jobs are to be found in these occupations).

---

[5] Note that this is a tight definition of 'skill-related' which excludes factors relating to applicants' personal attributes and to general competition among employers for the best applicants.

[6] As many as 40% of private sector establishments experiencing rapid growth in sales were recruiting at the time of the survey and some 28% of these recruiting establishments reported external skill shortages.

[7] The category of 'personal services' here includes vacancies for chefs and other catering occupations.

**5.19** As expected, the majority of external skill shortages were concentrated in the larger industries such as business services, wholesale and retail, manufacturing and health and social care (Table 5.2). However, construction stands out as having a disproportionately large share (13%) of external skill shortages relative to its 4% share of total employment, reflecting its heavy reliance on craft skills. By contrast, an industry like hotels and restaurants has a disproportionately large share of hard-to-fill vacancies but many of these reflect low pay, unsociable working hours and shortcomings in applicants' perceived personal qualities rather than scarcity of required skills. Hence the hospitality industry's share of external skill shortages does not exceed its employment share.

**5.20** Within each sector, the main areas of recruitment difficulty corresponded to predictably important occupations, for example, craft and operative vacancies in manufacturing, craft in construction, sales vacancies in the wholesale/retail sector, personal service vacancies in hospitality industries (hotels, restaurants and catering),[7] operators in transport and communications, clerical and secretarial vacancies in public administration, professional staff in education and associate professional vacancies in health and social work and business services (Table 5.3).

**Table 5.2: Total employment and estimated total vacancies, hard-to-fill vacancies and external skill shortages in England, analysed by sector**

|  | Total Employment England, June 1999(a) | SURVEY-BASED ESTIMATES: | | |
|---|---|---|---|---|
|  |  | Total unfilled vacancies | Total hard-to-fill vacancies | Total external skill shortages(c) |
| **Total numbers** | **20.04 mn** | **560000** | **255000** | **110000** |
|  | Percentages | | | |
| Manufacturing | 17 | 12 | 14 | 16 |
| Construction | 4 | 4 | 8 | 13 |
| Wholesale & Retail | 18 | 21 | 18 | 15 |
| Hotels & Restaurants | 6 | 10 | 11 | 6 |
| Transport & Communications | 6 | 6 | 7 | 8 |
| Financial Services | 5 | 4 | 3 | 4 |
| Business Services | 15 | 15 | 14 | 17 |
| Public Administration | 5 | 4 | 2 | 2 |
| Education | 8 | 5 | 4 | 4 |
| Health & Social Care | 10 | 12 | 14 | 10 |
| Other Services | 5 | 5 | 5 | 5 |
| Miscellaneous Industries(b) | 1 | 1 | 1 | 1 |
| **Total** | **100** | **100** | **100** | **100** |

(a) Not seasonally adjusted; excludes agriculture, forestry and fishing

(b) Includes mining and quarrying; electricity, gas and water supply

(c) See Table 5.1, Note b.

Sources: Employment: Labour Market Trends, November 1999, Table B16; Estimates of vacancies based on ECISD survey data.

**Figure 5.3: Total external skill shortages by sector**

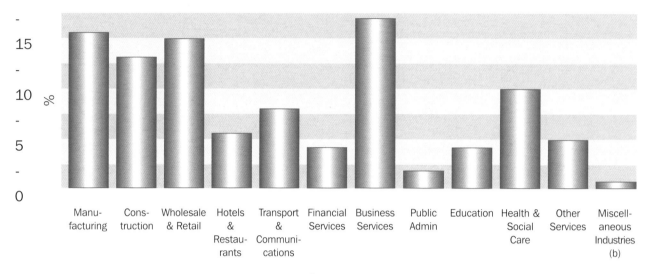

**Table 5.3: Distribution of external skill shortages by occupational area and sector**

| | Manufacturing | Construction | Wholesale, retail | Hotels, restaurants | Transport and communications | Financial services | Business services | Public administration | Education | Health and social work | Other services | Total (a) |
|---|---|---|---|---|---|---|---|---|---|---|---|---|
| | % of external skill shortages | | | | | | | | | | | |
| Managers/senior administrative | 9 | 1 | 8 | 4 | 7 | 5 | 10 | 8 | 24 | 3 | 8 | 7 |
| Professional | 7 | 2 | 2 | 0 | 2 | 6 | 18 | 16 | 32 | 6 | 7 | 8 |
| Associate professional/technical | 7 | 4 | 7 | 0 | 10 | 23 | 29 | 16 | 13 | 62 | 19 | 17 |
| Clerical/secretarial | 3 | 1 | 6 | 6 | 16 | 31 | 13 | 52 | 8 | 4 | 8 | 9 |
| Craft and skilled | 43 | 73 | 22 | 1 | 2 | 0 | 11 | 0 | 0 | 0 | 3 | 22 |
| Personal service | 0 | 0 | 2 | 62 | 1 | 0 | 7 | 7 | 20 | 23 | 51 | 11 |
| Sales | 9 | 11 | 43 | 3 | 4 | 35 | 7 | 0 | 3 | 1 | 2 | 13 |
| Operative and assembly | 20 | 3 | 7 | 0 | 55 | 0 | 4 | 0 | 0 | 1 | 0 | 9 |
| Other manual occupations | 2 | 4 | 1 | 24 | 3 | 0 | 1 | 0 | 0 | 1 | 2 | 3 |
| **Total** | **100** | **100** | **100** | **100** | **100** | **100** | **100** | **100** | **100** | **100** | **100** | **100** |

(a): Also includes two sectors for which results are not shown here: mining and quarrying and electricity and water supply

Base: All external skill shortages

## Skills sought for hard-to-fill vacancies

**5.21** As shown in Figure 5.4, the main types of skill which employers with external skill shortages found hard to obtain were vocational ('technical and practical') in nature (reported by almost half of establishments with such vacancies). These were followed by a range of generic skills: communication (31%), customer handling (29%), team-working (26%) and problem-solving (21%). Most of these generic skills were sought after to some extent in all occupational categories; however, concerns about inadequate communication and customer-handling skills were most commonly reported in relation to sales, personal service and clerical vacancies. Team-working skills were sought in particular for personal service, sales, craft and operator vacancies. Management skills featured prominently, not just in connection with managerial positions, but also for hard-to-fill vacancies in professional and associate professional areas. Lack of basic computing skills was reported as a problem mainly for clerical positions while lack of advanced IT skills was mainly associated with professional and associate professional vacancies (Table 5.4).

## Figure 5.4: Skills sought in connection with external skill shortages

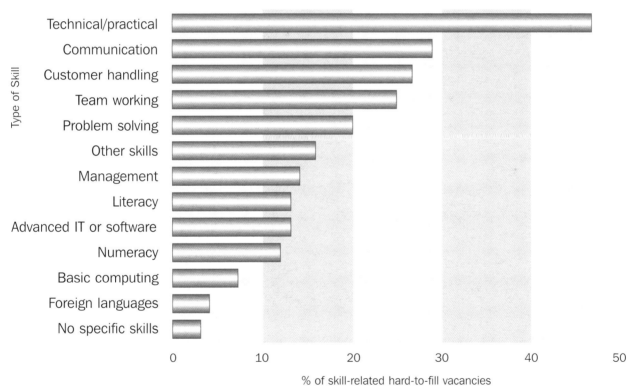

Base: All skill-related hard-to-fill vacancies (data refer to vacancy-weighted proportions of establishments)
Note: Respondents could cite more than one skill area associated with hard-to-fill vacancies.

**5.22** The high proportion of hard-to-fill vacancies requiring technical skills reflects strong demand from establishments seeking to fill craft, operative, associate professional and professional vacancies. As Table 5.5 shows, in these occupational areas technical skills were often sought without any reference to generic skill requirements. In addition, technical skills were sought in combination with generic skills for sizeable proportions of hard-to-fill vacancies in all occupational areas and particularly for clerical/secretarial vacancies. Generic skills were most likely to be sought in isolation from technical skills for sales vacancies. The generic category here includes basic numeracy and literacy skills which were most commonly cited as hard to find by establishments experiencing recruitment difficulties in clerical/secretarial and sales occupations.

**Table 5.4: Main skills sought in connection with external skill shortages, analysed by occupational area**

| Occupational area | Main skills sought (% of skill-related hard-to-fill vacancies in each occupational area) | Occupational area | Main skills sought (% of skill-related hard-to-fill vacancies in each occupational area) |
|---|---|---|---|
| Managers/ senior administrative | Management (49) | Associate professional/ technical | Technical/practical (49) |
| | Customer handling (36) | | Advanced IT/software (31) |
| | Technical/practical (34) | | Management (16) |
| | Problem-solving (33) | Sales | Communication (53) |
| Craft and skilled | Technical/practical (68) | | Customer handling (50) |
| | Team working (23) | | Team working (36) |
| | Communication (18) | Clerical/ secretarial | Communication (42) |
| Professional | Technical/practical (48) | | Customer handling (42) |
| | Advanced IT/software (25) | | Technical/practical (41) |
| | Problem-solving (20) | Operative and assembly | Technical/practical (49) |
| | Management (20) | | Communication (27) |
| Personal service | Customer handling (47) | | Team working (24) |
| | Technical/practical (38) | | |
| | Communication (37) | | |
| | Team working (36) | | |

Base: All skill-related hard-to-fill vacancies (data refer to vacancy-weighted proportions of establishments)
Notes: Respondents could cite more than one skill area associated with hard-to-fill vacancies.
Results for 'other manual' occupations not shown due to small cell sizes.

**Table 5.5: Type of skills sought by establishments reporting external skill shortages**

| | Technical skills only | Generic skills only | Technical and generic skills in combination | Other/non-specified types of skill | TOTAL |
|---|---|---|---|---|---|
| | % of skill-related hard-to-fill vacancies in each occupational area | | | | |
| Managers/senior administrative | 11 | 34 | 33 | 23 | 100 |
| Professional | 35 | 13 | 33 | 20 | 100 |
| Associate professional/technical | 43 | 9 | 25 | 22 | 100 |
| Clerical/secretarial | 20 | 25 | 40 | 15 | 100 |
| Craft and skilled | 50 | 13 | 22 | 15 | 100 |
| Personal service | 11 | 31 | 30 | 27 | 100 |
| Sales | 13 | 41 | 28 | 18 | 100 |
| Operative and assembly | 32 | 21 | 20 | 27 | 100 |

Base: All skill-related hard-to-fill vacancies (data refer to vacancy-weighted proportions of establishments).
Note: 'Technical skills' here comprise basic computer literacy, advanced IT and other technical/practical skills; 'Generic skills' comprise communication skills, customer handling skills, team working skills, problem solving skills, management skills, numeracy skills and literacy skills.
Results for 'other manual' occupations not shown due to small cell sizes.

## The commercial impact of external skill shortages

**5.23** The main reported consequences of skill-based recruitment problems were: difficulties meeting customer service objectives (cited by 60% of establishments with external skill shortages), delays in developing new products or services (44%), increased operating costs (42%) and loss of business to competitors (36%) (see Figure 5.5). These consequences were most severe in small establishments where the unfilled positions represented relatively large proportions of employment. However, longer-lasting vacancies in craft, associate professional and professional occupations were strongly associated with customer service problems and delays in introducing new products and services in establishments of all sizes. Loss of business or orders to competitors was often cited by establishments facing recruitment problems in managerial, professional, craft and sales areas. Difficulties meeting quality standards featured most strongly among the consequences of hard-to-fill vacancies in operator and personal service occupations (Table 5.6).

**5.24** Findings from the Employer Case Studies provided clear illustrations of these impacts. For example, in some engineering establishments shortages of electronics, software and design engineers had contributed to slowdowns in research and development activity and difficulties in responding to market demand. In financial services shortages of IT specialists and difficulties in filling senior management positions hindered some companies' business growth and disrupted customer service. In telecoms services shortages of telecommunications and software engineers had caused some firms to react slowly to business opportunities as well as lose a high proportion of management time to staff recruitment activity. In hospitality industries protracted vacancies among chefs and other kitchen staff led to revenue losses and poorer service and added to high labour turnover rates by increasing stress on other employees. In hospitals shortages of associate professional staff such as radiographers and physiotherapists directly contributed to longer waiting lists as well as to reductions in service quality.

**Figure 5.5: Impact of external skill shortages on establishment performance**

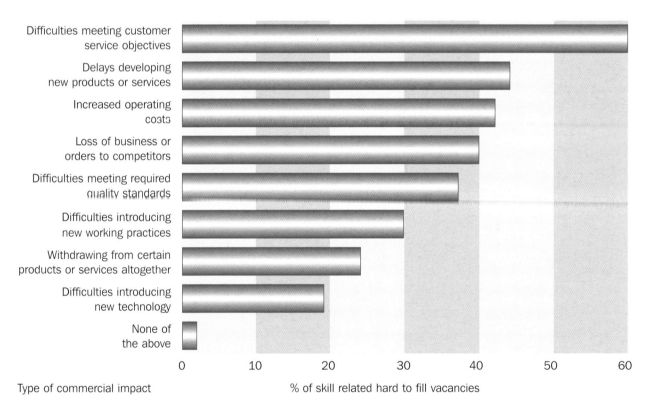

Type of commercial impact · % of skill related hard to fill vacancies

Base: All skill-related hard-to-fill vacancies (data refer to vacancy-weighted proportions of establishments).
Note: Respondents could cite more than one commercial impact of hard-to-fill vacancies.

**Table 5.6: Main impacts of external skill shortages on establishment performance**

| Occupational area | Main commercial impact (% of skill-related hard-to-fill vacancies in each occupational area) | Occupational area | Main commercial impact (% of skill-related hard-to-fill vacancies in each occupational area) |
|---|---|---|---|
| Managers/senior administrative | Customer service adversely affected (49) Delays to new product/service development (44) Loss of business/orders (37) | Associate professional/ technical | Delays to new product/service development (61) Customer service adversely affected (56) Increased operating costs (51) |
| Craft and skilled | Customer service adversely affected (75) Loss of business/orders (53) Increased operating costs (48) | Sales | Loss of business/orders (47) Customer service adversely affected (44) Quality standards not met (31) |
| Professional | Customer service adversely affected (62) Delays to new product/service development (51) Loss of business/orders (36) Increased operating costs (36) | Clerical/Secretarial | Customer service adversely affected (55) Delays to new product/ service development (38) Quality standards not met (36) Increased operating costs (36) |
| Personal service | Customer service adversely affected (48) Quality standards not met (43) Increased operating costs (38) | Operative and assembly | Customer service adversely affected (72) Increased operating costs (61) Quality standards not met (51) |

Base: All skill-related hard-to-fill vacancies (data refer to vacancy-weighted proportions of establishments).

Notes: Respondents could cite more than one commercial impact of hard-to-fill vacancies.

Results for 'other manual' occupations not shown due to small cell sizes.

## Summary

**5.25** This chapter has focussed on new survey evidence on the extent and nature of external skill shortages as reported by employers, that is, skill-related hard-to-fill vacancies explicitly attributed to a lack of job applicants with the required skills, qualifications or work experience. At the time of the survey (August-November, 1999), external skill shortages defined in this way affected about one in twelve establishments and represented about 43% of all hard-to-fill vacancies. The main causes of other types of recruitment difficulty were job seekers' lack of interest in particular kinds of jobs and low numbers of applicants with the required personal attributes in terms of attitudes and motivation.

**5.26** The main occupations associated with external skill shortages were those where relatively long periods of education and on-the-job training are needed to gain the required skills and knowledge, notably craft and skilled occupations (22% of all external skill shortages) and associate professional occupations (17%). The next most prominent occupations where external skill shortages were reported were sales (13%) and personal service occupations (11%).

**5.27** The industries most affected by external skill shortages were the craft-intensive construction and manufacturing sectors and two large service industries (finance and business services). As expected, the incidence of external skill shortages was substantially greater in large establishments than in small and medium-sized ones and was also greater in southern and eastern regions than in the Midlands or North of England.

**5.28** Many establishments seeking to fill craft, operative, associate professional and professional vacancies cited vocational (technical and practical) skills as hard to find without specific reference to generic skill requirements. In addition, technical skills were sought in combination with generic skills for sizeable proportions of hard-to-fill vacancies in all occupational areas and particularly for clerical/secretarial and managerial vacancies. Generic skills were most likely to be sought in isolation from technical skills for sales and personal service vacancies.

**5.29** Although external skill shortages affect a relatively small proportion of establishments at any point in time - 8% in 1999 - they have negative consequences for *one in four* of all establishments which are actually undertaking recruitment, particularly faster-growing establishments. The principal effects of such shortages are difficulties in meeting customer service objectives, delays in developing new products or services, increased operating costs and difficulties meeting required quality standards.

# REFERENCES

AGR (1997), *Graduate Salaries and Vacancies 1997 Survey,* Association of Graduate Recruiters, January.

AGR (1998), *Graduate Salaries and Vacancies 1998 Summer Update,* Association of Graduate Recruiters, June.

Arrow, K. and Capron, W. (1959), Dynamic shortages and price rises: the engineer-scientist case, *Quarterly Journal of Economics,* Vol. 73: 292-308.

Blank, D. and Stigler, G. (1959), *The Demand and Supply of Scientific Personnel,* New York: National Bureau of Economic Research.

Blake, N, Dods, J and Griffiths, S (2000), *Extent, Causes & Implications of Skills Deficiencies - Existing Survey Evidence and its use in the Analysis of Skills Deficiencies,* London: Business Strategies Ltd (forthcoming).

EMTA/EEF (1999), *The 1999 People Skills Scoreboard for Engineering,* Watford and London: Engineering and Marine Training Authority / Engineering Employers Federation.

Green, F. and Ashton, D. (1992), Skill shortage and skill deficiency - a critique, *Work, Employment & Society,* Vol. 6, No. 2: 287-301.

Hart, P. (1990), Skill shortages in the United Kingdom, NIESR Discussion Paper (Old Series), No. 169.

IFF (1998), *Skill Needs in Great Britain and Northern Ireland 1998,* Report to the Department for Education and Employment and the Training and Employment Agency, London: IFF Research Ltd.

IPD (1997), *'Over-qualified' and underemployed?,* Institute of Personnel and Development, London.

IRS (1995), Graduate recruitment and sponsorship: the 1995 IRS survey of employer practice, *Employee Development Bulletin,* No. 71, November.

IT NTO (1999), *Skills 99: IT Skills Summary,* Report to the Department of Trade and Industry, London: National Training Organisation for Information Technology, January.

Mann, R. and Junankar, S. (1998), 40 years on: how do companies respond to the CBI's Industrial Trends Survey?, *CBI Economic Situation Report,* Confederation of British Industry, November.

Mason, G. (1999), Engineering skills formation in Britain: cyclical and structural issues, Skills Task Force Research Paper 7, London: Department for Education and Employment.

Meager, N. (1986), Skill shortages again and the UK economy, *Industrial Relations Journal,* Vol. 17, No. 3.

# CHAPTER 6
## INTERNAL SKILL GAPS AND FUTURE SKILL REQUIREMENTS

## Introduction

**6.1** Many of the problems attributable to external skill shortages - as discussed in Chapter 5 - also arise as a result of skill deficiencies among *existing* employees in many organisations. In this chapter survey evidence on the extent, nature and commercial impacts of internal skill problems of this kind is reviewed. The chapter also looks at whether firms consider they have the skills necessary to meet future requirements. In many cases internal skill gaps are identified and recognised as such by employers. However, the chapter also considers the possibility that some skill gaps are 'latent' in nature, taking the form of unrecognised deficiencies in the skills required to compete effectively in rapidly changing world markets.

## Internal skill gaps

### Employer perceptions of current skill deficiencies

**6.2** One measure of internal skill gaps is the extent to which employers perceive their employees' current skills as insufficient to meet current business objectives. In 1998 some 15% of establishments in the SNIB survey identified skill shortcomings of this kind.[1] Another piece of evidence is a 1999 survey of engineering employers which found that just over a quarter of engineering establishments reported a gap between current workforce skills and the skills required to meet business objectives (EMTA/EEF 1999). In both the SNIB and EMTA/EEF surveys the main areas of deficiency which were identified embraced a wide range of technical and practical skills and shortcomings in generic skill areas such as computer literacy, communication skills, problem-solving skills and customer handling skills.

**6.3** Both these surveys had the disadvantage that respondents were asked to generalise about the adequacy of workforce skills as a whole in their establishments. In order to gain a more detailed understanding of skill gaps, the ESS asked employers to comment on an occupation-by-occupation basis about the extent to which employees were 'fully proficient at their current job'. The proportions of establishments reporting that all staff were fully proficient ranged from 52% (in the case of establishments employing sales staff) to 69% (of those employing professional staff) (Table 6.1). Just over a third (35%) of establishments reported a lack of full proficiency in two or more different occupational areas.

---

[1] In previous years the proportion acknowledging such problems had ranged between 12% (in 1994) and 21% (in 1995).

**Table 6.1: Employee proficiency levels in current jobs, analysed by occupation**

| | All staff fully proficient at current jobs | Nearly all staff proficient at current jobs | 'Over half' or fewer staff proficient at current jobs | Don't know | TOTAL | Establishments employing people in each occupation as % of all establishments |
|---|---|---|---|---|---|---|
| | % of establishments employing people in each occupation | | | | | |
| Managers/senior administrative | 67 | 24 | 8 | 1 | 100 | 98 |
| Professional | 69 | 24 | 5 | 2 | 100 | 39 |
| Associate professional/technical | 64 | 26 | 7 | 3 | 100 | 25 |
| Clerical/secretarial | 65 | 25 | 8 | 1 | 100 | 63 |
| Craft and skilled | 61 | 28 | 9 | 2 | 100 | 28 |
| Personal service | 56 | 30 | 12 | 2 | 100 | 23 |
| Sales | 52 | 33 | 14 | 2 | 100 | 34 |
| Operative and assembly | 57 | 30 | 10 | 3 | 100 | 18 |
| Other manual occupations | 65 | 24 | 9 | 2 | 100 | 28 |

Base: All establishments employing at least one person in respective occupations.

Note: The survey question on this topic asked respondents: 'What proportion of your existing staff at this establishment in (each occupation) would you regard as being fully proficient at their current job: all, nearly all, over half, some but under half, very few?' Follow-up questions about the percentage signified by an evaluation of 'nearly all' elicited a median score of 85% fully proficient (inter-quartile range 80%-90%); for an evaluation of 'over half' the equivalent percentage ratings had a median of 65% (inter-quartile range 60-70%).

6.4   Responses to follow-up questions suggested that in most cases where not all staff were regarded as fully proficient, employers were referring to relatively small proportions (10-20%) of employees in those occupations as lacking full proficiency.  However, in key occupations such as managers and professionals, even shortcomings on this scale could have damaging consequences for the firms or organisations involved.  For example, the employer case study of central and local government establishments found that over-spending on projects, inefficiencies in the use of IT and low staff morale were often attributed to weaknesses in the project management and communication skills of existing senior staff.  In some of the engineering case studies efforts to reorganise production systems and introduce new, more efficient working practices had been hindered by lack of commercial awareness and leadership skills among senior engineers.  In some of the banking and finance case studies, slow business development and 'inappropriate business decisions' were blamed on gaps in management skills.

**6.5** For purposes of analysis an 'internal skill gap' is defined as existing where lack of full proficiency (as perceived by employers) typically involved a third or more of staff in at least one occupational area. In all about one in five establishments fitted into this category. The proportions of establishments reporting skill gaps ranged from approximately 5% of those employing professionals to 14% of those employing sales staff (Table 6.1, Column 3). Skill gaps were least reported in very small establishments (employing less than 25 people) and in the education and construction sectors. The industries most affected were hospitality, wholesale and retail, manufacturing, transport and communications, financial services and public administration (Table 6.2).

**Table 6.2: Incidence of internal skill gaps, analysed by employee size-group and sector**

| By size of establishment: | Percent of establishments reporting internal skills gap (a) |
|---|---|
| 5-24 | 18 |
| 25-49 | 24 |
| 50-99 | 26 |
| 100-199 | 27 |
| 200-499 | 29 |
| 500-999 | 26 |
| 1000-plus | 26 |
| **TOTAL** | **20** |
| By sector: | Percent of establishments reporting internal skills gap (a) |
| Manufacturing | 21 |
| Construction | 16 |
| Wholesale & Retail | 21 |
| Hotels & Restaurants | 23 |
| Transport & Communications | 20 |
| Financial Services | 20 |
| Business Services | 18 |
| Public Administration | 20 |
| Education | 15 |
| Health & Social Care | 17 |
| Other Services | 21 |

Base: All establishments

(Mining and quarrying and Electricity and water not shown due to small cell sizes)

Note: (a) Refers to establishments where a third or more staff in at least one occupational area were not considered to be fully proficient (see Note to Table 6.1).

**6.6** The incidence of internal skill gaps differed from that of external skill shortages in several ways. Firstly, skill gaps were most commonly found in relatively low-skilled occupations such as sales, personal service and operative and assembly occupations (Table 6.1). By contrast, as shown above, external skill shortages were at their highest in craft and associate professional occupations which typically require relatively long periods of education and training in order to reach the required skill levels (Table 5.3). Secondly, some of the sectors most strongly affected by external skill shortages such as construction and business services did not rank highly in terms of skill gaps. Thirdly, private sector establishments with skill gaps were less likely than those with recruitment difficulties to be experiencing rapid growth in sales (Table 6.3). In general there was only a small degree of overlap between establishments reporting each kind of skill problem: only some 13% of establishments with internal skill gaps also reported having external skill shortages.[2]

**Table 6.3: Private sector establishments analysed by incidence of skill problems and changes in sales in previous 12 months**

| Change in sales | All private sector establishments | Private establishments with external skill shortages | Private establishments with internal skill gaps (a) |
|---|---|---|---|
| | **Percentages** | | |
| Increased a great deal | 16 | 23 | 18 |
| Increased a little | 33 | 33 | 34 |
| Stayed same | 25 | 21 | 21 |
| Decreased a little | 10 | 10 | 13 |
| Decreased a great deal | 4 | 3 | 5 |
| Don't know | 11 | 11 | 9 |
| **TOTAL** | **100** | **100** | **100** |

Base: All private sector establishments.

Note: (a) Refers to establishments where 'over half' or fewer of staff were assessed as being fully proficient at their current jobs in at least one occupation (see Note to Table 5.3).

**6.7** As Figure 6.1 shows, employers perceived internal skill gaps in terms of generic skill deficiencies (especially in communication, customer handling and team-working skills) ahead of the technical and practical skills which underlay many skill-related recruitment difficulties. However, it is notable that in every occupational area roughly a half to two thirds of establishments with skill gaps defined their problems in terms of employees lacking a desired *mix* of generic and vocational skills (Table 6.4).

---

[2] From the reverse perspective, only three out of ten establishments with external skill shortages also had internal skill gaps.

**Figure 6.1: Skills sought in connection with internal skill gaps**

|  |  |
|-------|-------|
| Communication | ~55 |
| Customer handling | ~51 |
| Team working | ~50 |
| Problem solving | ~45 |
| Technical/practical | ~44 |
| Management | ~36 |
| Basic computing | ~28 |
| Advanced IT or software | ~26 |
| Literacy | ~18 |
| Numeracy | ~17 |
| Foreign languages | ~9 |
| Other skills | ~9 |
| No specific skills | ~8 |

% of establishments with internal skills gaps

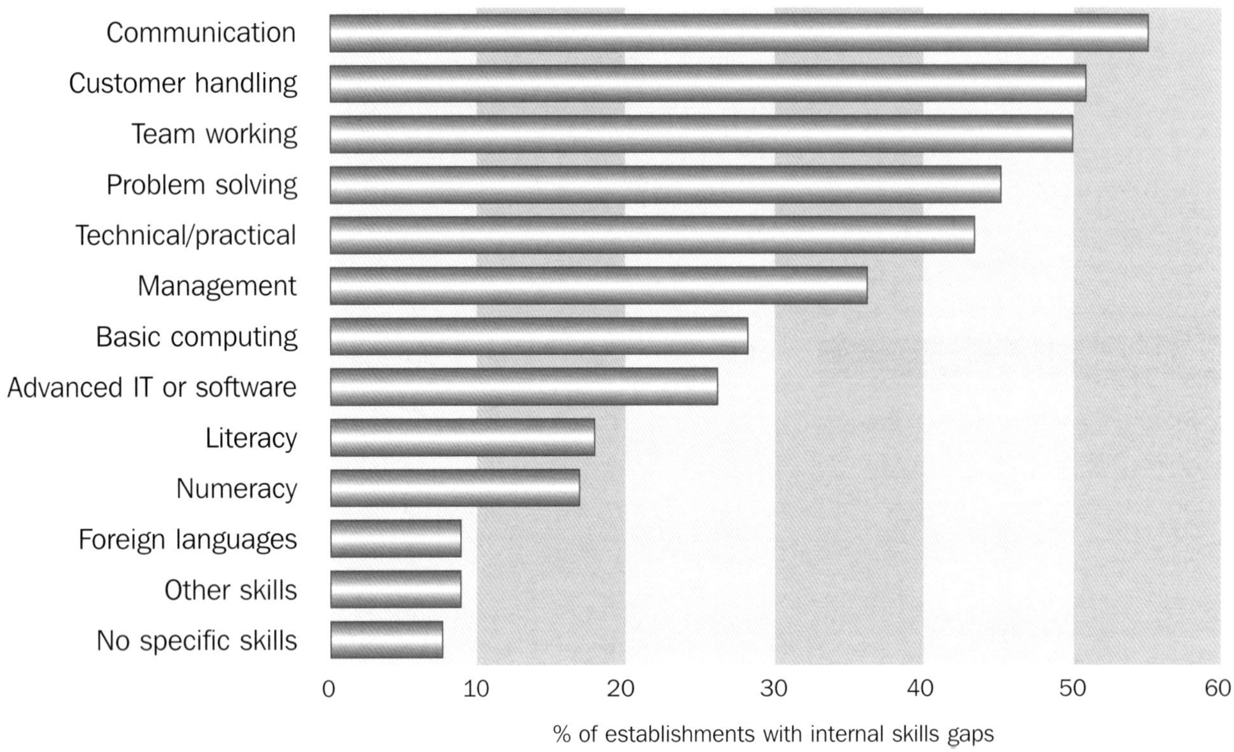

Base: All establishments with internal skill gaps
Note: Respondents could cite more than one skill area associated with internal skill gaps.

6.8  Technical and practical skills still ranked highest in craft, operator, professional and associate professional occupations.  But even in these occupations vocational skill gaps were paralleled by deficiencies in generic skills of different kinds (Table 6.5).  In managerial, personal service, sales and clerical occupations, deficiencies in communication and customer-handling skills were the areas of greatest concern.  In addition, employers reporting skill gaps identified problems with numeracy and literacy skills  in lower skill occupations, basic computing skills in clerical occupations, advanced IT skills in clerical, associate professional, professional and managerial occupations and management skills in professional and managerial occupations.[3]

---

[3]  See IER Survey Report, May 2000, Table 3.10.

## Table 6.4: Type of skills sought by establishments reporting internal skill gaps

| | Technical skills only | Generic skills only | Technical and generic skills in combination | Other/non-specified types of skill | TOTAL |
|---|---|---|---|---|---|
| | % of establishments reporting internal skill gaps in each occupational area | | | | |
| Managers/senior administrative | 8 | 27 | 58 | 7 | 100 |
| Professional | 12 | 17 | 64 | 8 | 100 |
| Associate professional/technical | 16 | 10 | 67 | 8 | 100 |
| Clerical/secretarial | 11 | 16 | 66 | 8 | 100 |
| Craft and skilled | 15 | 17 | 60 | 8 | 100 |
| Personal service | 5 | 39 | 46 | 10 | 100 |
| Sales | 7 | 40 | 45 | 8 | 100 |
| Operative and assembly | 12 | 22 | 57 | 9 | 100 |
| Other manual occupations | 10 | 33 | 48 | 10 | 100 |

Base: All establishments with internal skill gaps.

Note: 'Technical skills' here comprise basic computer literacy, advanced IT and other technical/practical skills; 'Generic skills' comprise communication skills, customer handling skills, team working skills, problem solving skills, management skills, numeracy skills and literacy skills.

6.9 The Employer Case Studies highlighted many examples of internal skill gaps relating to both generic and vocational skills. For example, many hotels and restaurants reported that some of their kitchen staff were lacking in both the required breadth of cooking skills and the 'customer awareness' needed to meet service standards. In telecoms services establishments, rapid changes in technologies and markets had exposed shortfalls in both technical skills and in the communication skills and business understanding required by technical staff in order to assume management responsibilities. In financial services and central/local government establishments, failure to use IT systems to their full potential was often attributed to gaps in communication and management skills as well as to shortfalls in specialist IT skills. In food processing efforts to improve production efficiency were hampered by poor communication skills among shopfloor workers (for example, in discussing and dealing with problems) and by relatively low levels of computer literacy.

**Table 6.5: Main skills sought in connection with external skill shortages, analysed by occupational area**

| Occupational Area | Main Skills Sought (% of establishments reporting that staff not fully proficient) | Occupational Area | Main Skills Sought (% of establishments reporting that staff not fully proficient) |
|---|---|---|---|
| Managers/ senior administrative | Management (53) Communication (52) Team working (45) | Craft and skilled | Technical/practical (51) Team working (37) Problem solving (35) |
| Professional | Technical/practical (43) Communication (42) Customer handling (39) | Personal service | Customer handling (62) Communication (55) Team working (50) |
| Associate professional/ technical | Technical/practical (44) Advanced IT/software (36) Communication (34) Team working (34) | Sales | Customer handling (60) Communication (51) Team working (43) |
| Clerical/ secretarial | Communication (42) Customer handling (42) Team working (38) | Operative and assembly | Technical/practical (43) Communication (43) Team working (41) |

Base: All establishments reporting lack of full proficiency among staff in each occupational area
Notes: Respondents could cite more than one skill area associated with internal skill gaps.
Results for 'other manual' occupations not shown due to small cell sizes.

6.10 Other industries provided examples of technically-based occupations where new demands are now being made in terms of generic skills. In engineering this was the case for professional engineers and craft-skilled workers who were now expected to display more commercial awareness and better communication and people-management skills. In health care associate professional staff such as physiotherapists are expected to combine vocational skills and knowledge with the ability to engage and motivate patients to take responsibility for their own rehabilitation.

## Causes of skill gaps

**6.11** Nearly half of respondents with internal skill gaps admitted that the problem was caused in part by their companies' 'failure to train and develop staff' - well ahead of the 31% blaming inability of the workforce to keep up with change (Figure 6.2). Acknowledgement of training deficiencies was ranked just ahead of the main factors driving up skill requirements, namely, the introduction of new working practices (46%), the development of new products (43%) and the introduction of new technology (37%). These changes contributed to skill shortcomings in nearly all occupational areas although lack of skills required for new product development particularly applied to managerial, professional and associate professional occupations (Table 6.6). Recruitment problems were cited as contributing to internal skill gaps in craft, operator and personal service occupations. In the case of craft skills these recruitment problems typically reflected external skill shortages. By contrast, in personal service occupations hard-to-fill vacancies typically derived from unattractive job conditions and job applicants' lack of desired personal attributes as much as lack of skills.

**Figure 6.2: Main causes of internal skill gaps cited by establishments with internal skill gaps**

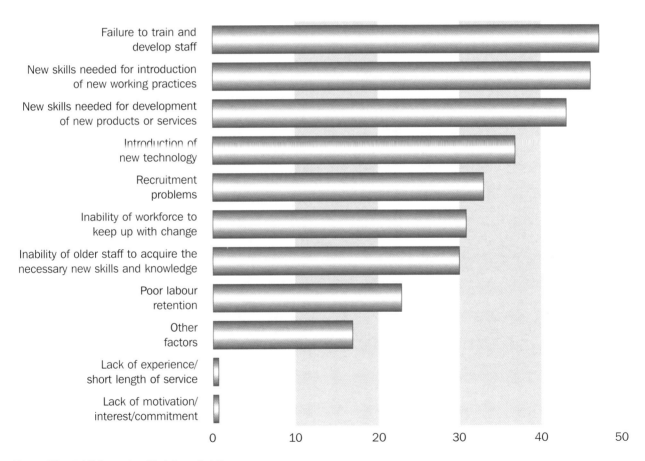

Base: All establishments with internal skill gaps
Note: Respondents could cite more than one reason for internal skill gaps

**Table 6.6: Main reasons for lack of full proficiency among existing staff, analysed by occupational area**

| Occupational Area | Main reasons for lack of full proficiency (% of establishments reporting that staff not fully proficient) | Occupational Area | Main reasons for lack of full proficiency (% of establishments reporting that staff not fully proficient) |
|---|---|---|---|
| Managers/senior administrative | Failure to train/develop staff (49) | Craft and skilled | New skills needed for new working practices (36) |
| | New skills needed for new working practices (46) | | Failure to train/develop staff (33) |
| | New skills needed for new products (39) | | Recruitment problems (30) |
| Professional | New skills needed for new working practices (43) | Personal service | Failure to train/develop staff (41) |
| | New skills needed for new products (43) | | New skills needed for new working practices (39) |
| | Failure to train/develop staff (40) | | Recruitment problems (37) |
| Associate professional/ technical Sales | Introduction of new technology (42) | Sales | Failure to train/develop staff (37) |
| | New skills needed for new products (42) | | New skills needed for new products (36) |
| | New skills needed for new working practices (33) | | New skills needed for new working practices (33) |
| Clerical/Secretarial | Introduction of new technology (43) | Operative and assembly | Failure to train/develop staff (37) |
| | New skills needed for new working practices (38) | | New skills needed for new working practices (34) |
| | New skills needed for new products (33) | | Recruitment problems (32) |
| | Failure to train/develop staff (33) | | Inability of workforce to cope with change (32) |

Base: All establishments reporting lack of full proficiency among staff in each occupational area
Notes: Respondents could cite more than one reason for lack of full proficiency.
Results for 'other manual' occupations not shown due to small cell sizes.

## The commercial impact of internal skill gaps

**6.12** The main effects of internal skill gaps on business performance were reported as difficulties in meeting customer service objectives and required quality standards along with increased operating costs (Figure 6.3). These problems were widely cited as a consequence of lack of full proficiency in nearly all occupations (Table 6.7). In addition, skill shortcomings among existing staff in managerial, professional, associate professional, clerical and craft occupations often hampered the introduction of new work practices while - as might be expected - lack of full proficiency in higher-level occupations contributed to delays in developing new products and services.[4]

**6.13** The Employer Case Studies suggest that problems caused by internal skill gaps often reflect a lack of forward planning for the new skills required to implement changes in product strategy or to upgrade existing products or services. In telecoms services the pace of change confronting the industry is so rapid that it is exceptionally difficult to plan ahead in a detailed way. In this industry the most serious uncertainty about the future relates not to technology changes but rather to the sheer difficulty of predicting the rate at which new services will be taken up. However, in other industries many internal skill gaps could in principle have been avoided or ameliorated if human resources or skill strategies had been more closely integrated with product strategies.

**6.14** For example, in some hospitality establishments changes in product strategy - such as an increase in conference hosting in hotels - had been launched without prior consideration of the new or additional workforce skills which would be required. In many engineering establishments product market or business strategy had been formulated with due account to manufacturing capability but with little attention to its implications for skills. Subsequently, training had been provided only after skill gaps had been identified in the course of attempting to implement the new product strategies. Similarly, in food processing there was little evidence of skills issues being considered in the course of developing product strategy. In some financial service establishments, forward planning of recruitment and training had been well integrated with decisions to move into new niche markets or to implement changes in work organisation but in other establishments sharp changes in business strategy had exposed serious internal gaps in the IT skills and leadership and other generic skills required for the new strategies to be successful.

---

[4] See IER Survey Report, May 2000, Table 3.11.

**Figure 6.3: Main impacts of internal skill gaps cited by establishments with internal skill gaps**

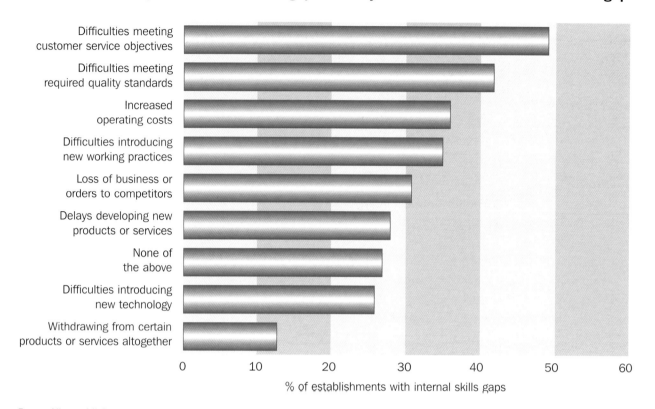

Base: All establishments with internal skill gaps

Note: Respondents could cite more than one commercial impact of internal skill gaps

**Table 6.7: Main impacts of lack of full proficiency on establishment performance, analysed by occupational area**

| Occupational Area | Main commercial impact (% of establishments reporting that staff not fully proficient) | Occupational Area | Main commercial impact (% of establishments reporting that staff not fully proficient) |
|---|---|---|---|
| Managers/senior administrative | Senior administrative Customer service adversely affected (44) Difficulties introducing new working practices (37) Increased operating costs (33) | Craft and skilled | Customer service adversely affected (42) Quality standards not met (42) Increased operating costs (40) |
| Professional | Customer service adversely affected (39) Increased operating costs (34) Quality standards not met (32) | Personal service | Customer service adversely affected (48) Quality standards not met (46) Increased operating costs (26) |
| Associate professional/ technical Sales | Delays in new product/ service development (34) Customer service adversely affected (33) Quality standards not met (29) | Sales | Customer service adversely affected (47) Loss of business/ orders (40) Quality standards not met (32) |
| Clerical/Secretarial | Secretarial Customer service adversely affected (38) Quality standards not met (33) Difficulties introducing new working practices (33) | Operative and assembly | Increased operating costs (45) Customer service adversely affected (44) Quality standards not met (42) |

Base: All establishments reporting lack of full proficiency among staff in each occupational area
Notes: Respondents could cite more than one commercial impact of lack of full proficiency.
Results for 'other manual' occupations not shown due to small cell sizes.

**Are skill problems under-reported?**

6.15 What are the implications of these findings for an overall assessment of skill imbalances in the British economy? The analysis presented in the Chapter suggests that approximately one in three survey respondents recognised that their establishments had skill problems of one kind or another. Taking care to avoid double-counting, this group of establishments breaks down as follows:

- 20% of establishments which reported internal skill gaps as defined above, namely, a lack of full proficiency affecting a third or more of employees in at least one occupational area

- another 7% of establishments which reported internal skill shortcomings which affected a sizeable minority (15% or more) of their entire workforce[5]

- another 5% of establishments which did not report internal skill problems of any kind but which did report having external skill shortages

6.16 Taken at face value, this suggests that - although skill deficiencies have serious consequences for the establishments affected, including some of the faster-growing ones - workforce skills are not a problem area for a majority (two thirds) of employers. However, the Employer Case Studies suggest that survey-based estimates may well understate the extent of the problem. Recall that case study investigations were carried out in 95 establishments in seven different manufacturing and service industries. Just under 85% of these establishments reported having internal skill gaps and many of these also faced external skill shortages at the time of the case study visits. In part this finding may be explicable by the fact that - having agreed to take part in case study investigations - these establishments have demonstrated a particular interest in skills issues and do not constitute a representative sample of establishments from the industries concerned. But it also suggests that when researchers have access to a range of respondents in establishments and are able to probe the initial responses given to questions, then many more skill problems are likely to be uncovered than would typically be identified through structured interviews with single respondents (as in the telephone and face-to-face surveys from which our main body of data were derived).

6.17 The Employer Case Studies also point to another reason why the estimate of one in three establishments with skill deficiencies is likely to understate the extent of the problem, namely, the fact that not all skill shortcomings are necessarily recognised as such by employers. For example, in some hotels and restaurants, researchers observed poor service being given to customers in departments where no skill problems had been reported. They also encountered very little awareness by hotel managers of the negative effects on customer service of their staff lacking foreign language skills. In the food processing case studies there were examples of machinery breakdowns being dealt with very slowly but without any recognition of the underlying skills issues. In both hospitality and financial services researchers identified problems of sub-optimal use of IT equipment which were partly skills-related but again not recognised as such by managers. In engineering some of the weaker-performing establishments appeared to suffer from a lack of strategic vision among senior managers, something which would not be reported as a skill problem.

---

[5] This estimate is based on calculations of employment-weighted skill proficiency scores for all surveyed establishments (see IER Survey Report, May 2000, Section 3.3)

**6.18** Further grounds for concluding that imbalances between skills supply and demand affect far more than a third of employers emerged from survey responses to a forward-looking question asking employers about the *future* problems they anticipated occurring as a result of skill shortcomings in their workforces. Almost half of all establishments in the survey cited at least one skills-related problem as likely to occur in the next two or three years, in particular, difficulties in meeting customer service and quality objectives and in keeping costs down. These concerns about future skill constraints on performance were frequently associated with employers' efforts to respond to competitive market pressures by developing new higher added value product strategies and/or making improvements in product quality and production efficiency. The survey findings - supported by case studies - suggest that, in the process of making such changes, hitherto latent skill gaps are gradually revealed in large numbers of establishments across the economy.[6]

**Forward-looking business strategies and future skill imbalances**

**6.19** Some 46% of establishments which did not report current skill gaps still anticipated at least one kind of skill problem in the future (Figure 6.4). One explanation for this may be that the more proficient establishments have relatively high expectations of future skill needs. Other findings show that the private sector establishments most likely to anticipate future problems were those which had experienced recent rapid *change* in sales or market share. As illustrated in Figure 6.5, the proportions of establishments expecting future problems due to skill shortcomings were typically highest where recent sales had either increased or declined and lowest where annual sales had remained unchanged.

**Figure 6.4: Current skill proficiency and anticipated future problems arising from skill shortcomings**

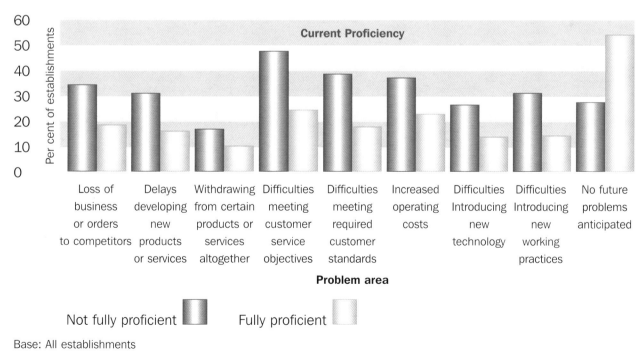

Base: All establishments

---

[6] Another way to assess the extent of latent skill gaps is to compare the current supply of skills against the notional demand for skills that would arise in the future if all establishments attempted to raise their strategic goals and performance towards those of the best performing establishments. Preliminary analysis of evidence from the face-to-face survey of establishments suggests that concerted efforts to move towards 'best practice' in this way would reveal a host of hitherto unperceived skill deficiencies (see Hogarth, 2000)

**6.20** These findings suggest that imbalances between future skill requirements and skill supplies are likely to be far greater than those implied by responses to questions about current skill gaps. They also suggest that the majority of establishments anticipating future skill-related problems can be divided into two categories: (1) high-performing establishments which maintain high aspirations as to future skill requirements; (2) weaker performers which have experienced recent declines in sales and/or market share and which recognise the need for skill levels to improve. This polarisation between establishments seeking to build on recent business success and those reacting to commercial setbacks also emerges from analysis of the relationship between product strategies and skill requirements, to which we now turn.

**Figure 6.5: Anticipated commercial problems due to future skill shortcomings, analysed by recent change in sales**

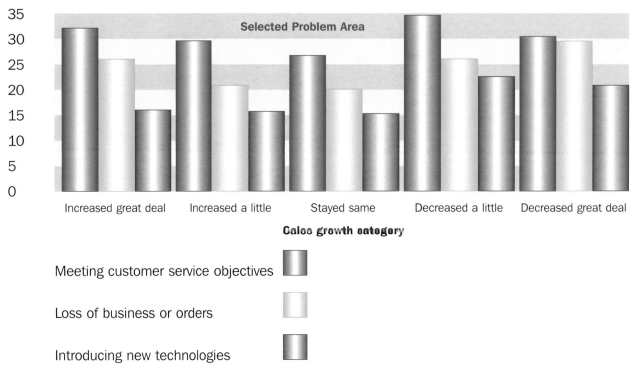

Base: All establishments anticipating future commercial problems due to skill shortcomings.

Note: Vertical axis shows percent of establishments in each growth category expecting designated problems.

## Product strategies and skill gaps

**6.21** During the 1980s and early 1990s comparisons of matched samples of British and Continental European establishments suggested that, in a range of different industries, a majority of British producers had settled on relatively low quality, low value added product strategies consistent with a low-skilled workforce (Prais, 1995). The extent to which such strategies are sustainable ultimately depends on the magnitude of competitive market pressures to move to higher value added product strategies. In some industries such as food processing, where there is a strong domestic market for standardised products, a product strategy based on low-skill, low value added bulk production may well be a viable strategy into the foreseeable future for many firms. However, in many other industries such as engineering, British firms have long faced severe competitive pressure from mass producers of standardised goods in lower-wage countries which has obliged them to refocus production towards small- and medium-batch production of higher value added products (Mason, van Ark and Wagner, 1996).

**6.22** The employer case studies carried out in a range of manufacturing and service industries - including telecoms services, financial services, hotels and food processing as well as engineering - show that product market competition is now so intense as to force a large proportion of companies to make strategic changes in product mix and/or their use of technology and work organisation in order to survive. These strategic changes in turn often rely on widespread skills upgrading for successful implementation. However, as described above (Paragraphs 6.11-6.12), in many companies the formulation of human resourcing and skills strategy tends to lag behind changes in product strategy, work organisation and production methods or service delivery. In this context hitherto unrecognised gaps emerge between current skill levels and those required for future success in competitive markets.

**6.23** The ESS found about four in ten private sector establishments reported efforts to move into new higher quality product or service areas with higher profit margins.[7] Table 6.8 shows that definite plans to move to higher quality product/service areas were most common among establishments where recent sales had either increased or decreased a great deal. It also shows that the proportion of establishments which definitely had no plans at all to move up-market was highest among those establishments which had experienced sharp declines in sales and lowest among the fastest-growing establishments. On balance, therefore, it is the better-performing establishments which are in the forefront of moves to higher quality product strategies, seeking to build on past success. The weaker performers appear to be polarised between establishments responding to market pressures for strategic change and those which, for one reason or another, intend to persevere with their current product strategy.

---

[7] The percentages refer to establishments which described the following statement as 'very applicable' or 'fairly applicable' to their operations: 'We are implementing, or are about to implement, plans to move into new higher quality product or service areas with higher profit margins'

**Table 6.8: Plans to move into higher product/service areas, analysed by recent change in sales**

| Degree of applicability to move into higher product/service area | Sales growth (last 12 months) | | | | |
|---|---|---|---|---|---|
| | Increased a great deal | Increased a little | Stayed the same | Decreased a little | Decreased a great deal |
| Very applicable | 23.2 | 16.2 | 13.4 | 13 | 18.9 |
| Fairly applicable | 22.2 | 25.2 | 18.8 | 21 | 17.9 |
| Not very applicable | 20.3 | 21.3 | 21.8 | 24 | 15.4 |
| Not at all applicable | 34.3 | 37.3 | 46 | 42.1 | 47.8 |

Base: All private sector establishments
Note: Degrees of applicability refer to the following statement about establishment: 'We are implementing, or about to implement, plans to move into new higher quality product or service areas with higher profit margins.'

## Skills needed for higher-quality product strategies

**6.24** It is firms seeking to move up-market in product strategy together with those planning to improve the quality of existing products and services that are most likely to identify new skill needs arising in the future. As many as 93% of all establishments seeking to upgrade quality in some way cited at least one 'new or additional' skill which would be required in order to meet their objectives (Figure 6.6). Generic skills, principally team-working, customer-handling and communication skills, were highest on the list but large proportions of establishments also cited technical/practical skills (55%), basic computer literacy skills (49%) and advanced IT/software skills (39%). Very strikingly, some 42% of respondents placed literacy and numeracy skills in this category of 'new or additional' skills which were required, which provides strong support for our concerns about basic skill deficiencies expressed in Chapter 3.[8]

**6.25** As Table 6.9 shows, the great majority of establishments seeking to move to higher value-added product strategies and/or improve the quality of existing products and services specified their new or additional skill requirements in terms of *combinations of generic and vocational skills*. These skill sets have much in common with those sought in order to fill recognised internal skill gaps (Table 6.5). It is possible that some survey respondents were merely paying lip-service to fashionable skill concerns during the interviews. However, the findings are supported by case study evidence on new skill requirements resulting from company responses to competitive market pressures in a variety of industries.

[8] In terms of sectoral distribution, the proportions of establishments citing a need for new or additional basic skills were highest in hotels and restaurants (55%) and wholesale/retailing (51%). However, the equivalent proportions were no lower than 39% in any other industry. Note that the proportion of employers concerned about new or additional basic skills far exceeds those reporting current deficiencies in such skills (about 5% of all establishments, similar to the incidence of current basic skills problems identified in previous SNIB surveys).

**Figure 6.6: New or additional skills required to move into higher quality product or service areas**

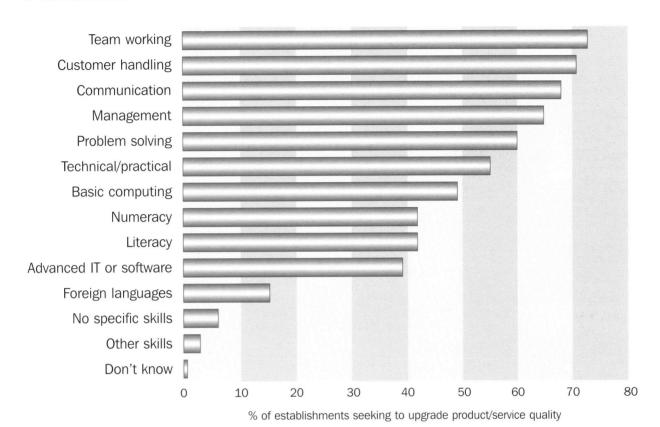

% of establishments seeking to upgrade product/service quality

Base: All establishments moving into higher quality product/service areas and/or seeking to improve quality of existing products/services

Note: Respondents could cite more than one new or additional skill requirement

6.26 For example, in telecoms services many employers confronted with high levels of uncertainty about future market trends see a need to develop 'hybrid' skills that combine technical expertise, market knowledge, business management skills and the ability to 'get to know' and understand business customers' telecommunications needs. In financial services future skill requirements are typically defined to cover a mix of vocational and generic skills (eg IT expertise and/or specialist financial knowledge combined with good inter-personal and team-working skills). In hotels and restaurants the growth of Internet-based marketing, sales and reservations activities has greatly added to existing needs for staff with good IT skills as well as the communication and inter-personal skills needed to relate to customers. In engineering the speeding-up of 'product life cycles' means that companies manufacturing low volume, high value added products may have to adapt quickly to 'maturing' markets and acquire the very different mixes of vocational and generic skills which are needed to compete effectively in higher-volume, low-cost production of more standardised goods.

**Table 6.9: Types of new or additional skills required to move into higher quality product or service areas**

| | Technical skills only | Generic skills only | Technical and generic skills in combination | Other/non-specified types of skill | TOTAL |
|---|---|---|---|---|---|
| **By size of establishment:** | % of establishments seeking to move into higher quality product or service areas | | | | |
| 5-24 | 6 | 17 | 68 | 8 | 100 |
| 25-49 | 5 | 14 | 73 | 8 | 100 |
| 50-99 | 5 | 13 | 75 | 7 | 100 |
| 100-199 | 3 | 11 | 80 | 5 | 100 |
| 200-499 | 2 | 10 | 82 | 5 | 100 |
| 500-999 | 5 | 7 | 82 | 6 | 100 |
| 1000-plus | 2 | 10 | 82 | 5 | 100 |
| **TOTAL** | **6** | **16** | **70** | **8** | **100** |
| **By sector:** | % of establishments seeking to move into higher quality product or service areas | | | | |
| Manufacturing | 7 | 12 | 71 | 10 | 100 |
| Construction | 8 | 10 | 73 | 9 | 100 |
| Wholesale & Retail | 5 | 20 | 67 | 8 | 100 |
| Hotels & Restaurants | 3 | 32 | 56 | 9 | 100 |
| Transport & Communications | 4 | 17 | 70 | 0 | 100 |
| Financial Services | 5 | 12 | 77 | 6 | 100 |
| Business Services | 7 | 10 | 76 | 8 | 100 |
| Public Administration | 6 | 8 | 77 | 9 | 100 |
| Education | 9 | 9 | 75 | 6 | 100 |
| Health & Social Care | 5 | 19 | 69 | 7 | 100 |
| Other Services | 5 | 16 | 73 | 6 | 100 |

Base: All establishments moving into higher quality product/service areas and/or seeking to improve quality of existing products/services.

Note: 'Technical skills' here comprise basic computer literacy, advanced IT and other technical/practical skills; 'Generic skills' comprise communication skills, customer handling skills, team working skills, problem solving skills, management skills, numeracy skills and literacy skills.

**6.27** Similar responses about the need for new or additional skills were made by establishments which had no plans to improve product quality but did plan to achieve higher efficiency. In general, therefore, the high level of awareness of the new or additional skills required to move to a higher value added product strategy or meet higher quality and efficiency standards goes a long way to explaining why nearly half of all establishments in the survey anticipated problems arising in the next two or three years due to skill shortcomings among their employees.

**Figure 6.7: Constraints on moving to higher valued added product areas, analysed by recent change in sales**

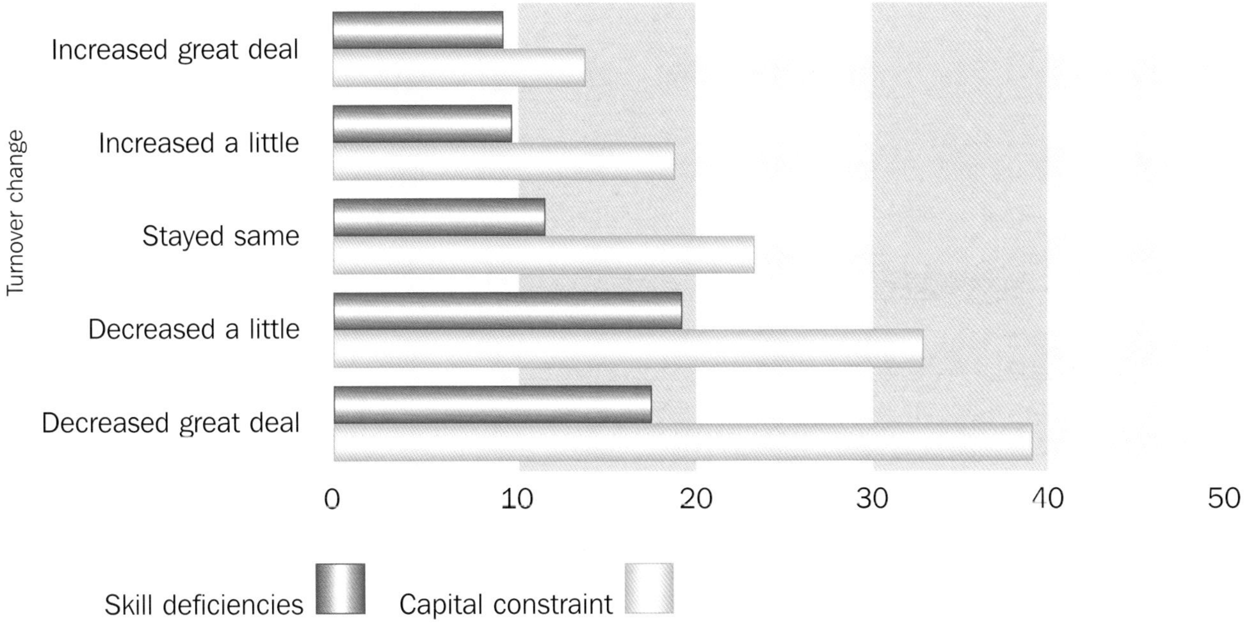

Base: All establishments not moving into higher quality product/service areas.
Note: Percentages refer to establishments who said the following statements were 'very' or 'fairly applicable' to them:
(a) 'We would like to move into new, higher quality product or service areas but we cannot afford the high level of capital investment required' (b) 'We would like to move into new, higher quality product or service areas but we lack the required skills in the workforce'.

6.28 In an effort to probe the relationship between product strategies and skills still further, those establishments which had no plans to move up-market were asked if they wished to move into new, higher quality product areas but were constrained from doing so by either financial or skill constraints. The results presented in Figure 6.7 show that skill constraints were generally outweighed by financial constraints and particularly so in the case of establishments which had recently experienced a fall in sales. In this context skills are at most regarded as a second order problem. Indeed, as described above, the evidence from case studies of establishments suggests that, when changes in product strategy do occur, they are often undertaken without much prior consideration of the new skills which will be required. Subsequently, internal skill gaps may be recognised and steps taken to try and solve the problems. In some cases these efforts are expected to succeed; in other cases concerns about future skill shortcomings remain (as captured in the survey results).

## Summary

**6.29** This chapter has focussed on new survey evidence on the extent and nature of internal skill gaps (defined as occurring where one third or more of existing staff in a particular occupation lack full proficiency at their current jobs). Skill gaps of this kind were recognised by employers in about one in five of all establishments. The degree of overlap between internal skill deficiencies and external recruitment difficulties was relatively small. In contrast to external skill shortages, internal skill gaps tended to occur in less-skilled occupations such as sales, personal service and operative and assembly occupations. There was also far less emphasis on scarcity of vocational (technical and practical) skills in isolation: the majority of establishments with internal skill gaps defined their problems in terms of employees lacking a desired *mix* of generic and vocational skills.

**6.30** Almost half of establishments with skill gaps acknowledged that these were partly due to their own failure to train and develop staff. The main factors driving up skill requirements were the introduction of new working practices, the development of new products and the introduction of new technology. The main impacts of internal skill gaps on business performance were similar to those attributed to external recruitment problems, that is, difficulties in meeting customer service objectives and required quality standards along with increased operating costs.

**6.31** In total roughly two thirds of all establishments did not report either skill-based recruitment difficulties or any serious skill gaps among existing staff. However, the Employer Case Studies suggest that there are no grounds for complacency about skill imbalances. Firstly, case study researchers found that when interviews of a probing nature are carried out with a wide range of respondents in individual establishments, the reported incidence of skill deficiencies is markedly higher than suggested by responses to short, structured surveys. Secondly, the case study researchers noted that some current skill gaps pass unrecognised by employers.

**6.32** In addition, other survey findings point to *potentially serious mismatches between skills supply and demand in the future.* Almost half of all establishments anticipated that commercial problems would arise in the next two or three years as a result of shortfalls in skills. The majority of these establishments expecting future skill-related problems fell into two categories: (1) high-performing establishments which maintain high aspirations as to future skill requirements; (2) weaker performers which have experienced recent declines in sales and/or market share and which recognise the need for skill levels to improve.

**6.33** A key factor driving up skill requirements in a range of manufacturing and service industries is the intensity of product market competition which forces many companies to make strategic changes in product mix and/or their use of technology and work organisation in order to survive. These strategic changes in turn often rely on widespread skills upgrading for successful implementation. However, as the case study evidence shows, in many companies the formulation of human resourcing and skills strategy tends to lag behind changes in product strategy, work organisation and production methods or service delivery. In this context hitherto latent and unrecognised skill gaps now appear to be emerging on a large scale and in a wide variety of industries.

**6.34** The skill requirements specified by the great majority of establishments seeking to move to higher value added product strategies and/or improve the quality of existing products and services confirm the growing importance of generic skills for business performance - principally team-working, customer-handling and communication skills. However, they also demonstrate the continuing importance of vocational (technical and practical) skills which were often sought in combination with improved generic skills. Very strikingly, about four in ten respondents seeking to upgrade product or service quality in some way said that new or additional literacy and numeracy skills would also be required, thus confirming the prevalence of deficiencies in basic skills.

## REFERENCES

EMTA/EEF (1999), *The 1999 People Skills Scoreboard for Engineering,* Watford and London: Engineering and Marine Training Authority / Engineering Employers Federation.

Hogarth, T (2000), *The Employers Skills Case Studies - Synthesis Report,* DfEE (forthcoming).

Mason, G., van Ark, B. and Wagner, K. (1996), Workforce skills, product quality and economic performance' in A. Booth, D. Snower (eds) *Acquiring Skills: Market Failures, their Symptoms and Policy Responses,* Cambridge: Cambridge University Press, 1996.

Prais, S. (1995), *Productivity, Education and Training: An International Perspective,* Cambridge: Cambridge University Press.

# CHAPTER 7

## MARKET SIGNALS - WHAT EARNINGS AND THE NATURE OF THE UNEMPLOYED TELL US ABOUT WHERE SKILLS ARE NEEDED

## Introduction

**7.1** The ESS found that roughly half of all employers facing skill-related recruitment difficulties are prepared to raise wages for those jobs where they are having difficulty in attracting the skills they need. This should help to widen pay differentials between jobs where skills are in demand and those with lower levels of demand (assuming no offsetting changes in other things such as the supply of skills). It should also mean that the rates of return to the skills most in demand would increase relative to those least needed (assuming the costs of acquiring those skills did not change). One aim of this chapter is to investigate the rates of return to various levels and types of skills as proxied by qualifications and assess what this tells us about where we could most usefully invest future provision to raise skill levels.

**7.2** Returns to various skills are not only determined by their relative scarcity. Returns are also determined by such factors as the amount of learning needed to acquire the skill - higher future wages being a major incentive for individuals to bear the cost of such learning. In many instances returns to skills also reflect the desirability of the jobs (e.g. the stressful nature of work as an air traffic controller is a major factor in the high wages available) and the probability of success in particular jobs (e.g. the high wages available to a small minority of top entertainers).

**7.3** Much of the research on rates of return, while offering very useful evidence on what level and type (academic or vocational) of qualification generates the best return, tells us less about which subjects of study provide the best returns. This chapter, therefore, looks at available evidence on trends in wage differentials by qualification and occupation to try and shed further light on trends in relative demand for skills.

**7.4** A final set of evidence considered in this chapter focusing on market signals is what trends in relative unemployment tell us about the skills most and least in demand. Changes in the relative unemployment rate of individuals with different skills (as proxied by their level of qualification or previous occupation) at similar points in the economic cycle indicates the extent to which those skills are more or less in demand in the labour market.

# The rate of return to skills

**7.5**   The best type evidence for identifying skill priorities is that which shows the areas where the rates of return are highest.  It is in these areas that further investment is likely to be the most beneficial to the economy.  As stated in Chapter 1, the ideal would be to measure the marginal rate of return to particular skills in the widest sense (the social rate of return).  This would give the best assessment of the overall cost of such investment and the best measure of the return to both individuals and society as a whole.  It would best identify those skills most likely to produce the highest future return (i.e. at the margin).  However, much of the research, particularly that related to the UK, is based on private rates of return and calculated on an average rather than marginal basis.

**7.6**   Furthermore, in common with a significant proportion of research on skills, findings do not relate directly to skills but to proxy measures thereof.  The length of time spent in full-time education is the most common proxy used in studies to estimate rates of return whilst qualifications are often used to estimate returns.  Elsewhere in the report we have discussed at length the strengths and weaknesses of using qualifications as a proxy for skills.  In identifying the areas where returns are highest, the research is able to distinguish between returns to different types and levels of qualifications.

## Returns to academic and vocational qualifications

**7.7**   The evidence on which type of qualifications produce the best rates of return is not conclusive. Research by Robinson (1997) pointed to much higher returns to academic qualifications than to 'equivalent' vocational qualifications.  For example, he found that men with two or more A-levels earned on average about 11% more than men with OND/ONC or BTEC National qualifications with the corresponding difference for women being 10%.  However, this research did not control for ability or family background - both of which have been shown to have a strong impact on rates of return to some academic qualifications - nor did it take account of the higher opportunity costs of gaining academic qualifications.  Hence it tends to inflate the returns to academic courses.  (Dearden, 1999).

**7.8**   Psacharopoulos (1994) estimated social rates of return to academic and vocational qualifications based on 32 studies of developing countries.  He found the social returns to academic qualifications were around 15.5% per annum and those for vocational qualifications were 11.7% per annum.  By contrast, Bennell (1996) questioned Psacharopoulos's methodology and, using similar data for developing countries, estimated that the social rates of return to academic and vocational were almost identical (13.3% and 13.1% respectively).

**7.9**   Previous studies of the returns to academic and vocational qualifications in the UK have tended to ignore the complex routes many people take in acquiring vocational qualifications.  Whilst academic qualifications are usually gained through well-established routes (e.g. GCSEs - A-level - Degree), the routes taken to achieve vocational qualifications are much less standardised.  Furthermore, focussing on the highest vocational or academic qualification achieved and failing to disentangle the different qualifications achieved along the way makes it hard to develop an accurate picture of the rates of return to specific qualifications (whether they be academic or vocational).

**7.10** In general, research comparing the returns to academic and vocational qualifications has tended not to allow for differences in the length of time needed to achieve given levels and types of qualification. For example, for several levels of qualification, the time required for full-time academic study is generally longer than the study time associated with part-time vocational routes. These differences need to be taken into account by calculating estimates of the annual rate of return to different qualifications based on the average number of years taken to gain each qualification. An analysis which estimates rates of return to individual qualifications is best suited to identifying priority areas for investment. It would also be desirable to take due account of differences in the opportunity costs (foregone wages) of gaining given levels of qualification through full-time and part-time routes.

**Returns to different levels of academic and vocational qualification**

**7.11** Recent research at the Institute of Fiscal Studies (IFS) and the Centre for Economic Performance (CEP) using data from the National Child Development Survey (NCDS), International Adult Literacy Survey (IALS) and Labour Force Survey (LFS) has made considerable progress in the analysis of relative rates of return to different types of qualifications (Dearden et al, 2000). The research finds relatively high returns for most academic qualifications for both men and women but particularly for women. In summary the findings are:

- GCSEs/ "O" levels produce a return of 12-21% for men and 10-19% for women[1]

- GCE "A" levels produce an additional 15-18% return for men and an additional 18-23% for women

- First degrees produce an additional 10-28% return for men and an additional 21-26% for women

**7.12** The returns to Level 3 vocational qualifications are generally lower than those accruing to their academic equivalents such as A-levels. For example, the estimated return to males for gaining an ONC/OND is 7-12% and for females 8%. The return for males holding the City & Guilds higher and advanced qualifications are estimated at 4-7% and 7-10% respectively.

**7.13** However, in contrast to previous UK research, this new evidence suggests that the rate of return to vocational qualifications at NVQ Level 3 or higher bear comparison with their academic equivalents if due account is taken of the different lengths of time required to obtain each new qualification. For example, if it is assumed that it takes a part-time student an average 11/4 years of full-time equivalent study to complete an ONC/OND compared to 2 years for an A-level, then the annualised rate of return for an ONC/OND of 51/2-91/2% pa for men is comparable to A-levels (71/2-9%). However, the same is not true for women where equivalent estimates of rates of return are 9-111/2% pa for A-levels and 61/2% for an ONC/OND.[2]

---

[1] The spread reflects the range of findings dependent on which data set is used - NCDS, IALS or LFS

[2] These results are clearly very sensitive to assumptions made about the length of time taken to acquire qualifications. Dearden et al, 2000 estimate that it can take between 0.6 to 2 years of full-time equivalent study to acquire an ONC/OND, which yields an average study time of around 1.25 years. The lower duration is based on an employee being released for one day a week by their employer in order to attend classes over a 2-3 year period.

**7.14** The same is true of the rate of return to HNC/HND qualifications compared to first degrees, at least for men. The estimated returns to HNC/HND's for men range between 6-22%. However, the upper estimate is based on a very small sample and is better discounted giving a range of between 6-15%. Assuming an average full-time equivalent study time again of 11/4 years, this gives an annualised rate of return of 5-12% which compares favourably with the estimated rate of return enjoyed by males gaining first degrees. Estimates based on LFS data point to a return for women gaining HNC/HND qualifications of roughly 9% (an annual rate of return of 7% pa).[3]

**7.15** The largest rate of return for all qualifications is gained by those acquiring professional qualifications, though a lack of information on the precise nature of these qualifications and possible data contamination with degree level qualifications means these findings should be treated with some caution. For men the rate of return for a professional qualification ranges from 15-35% and for women 20-40%.

**7.16** However, while annualised rates of return to vocational qualifications at Level 3 and above are comparable to those gained through academic qualifications, there is little evidence of good rate of returns for vocational qualifications below that level. The Dearden et al study reveals no return to lower level NVQs for either gender. For men, there is no evidence of a good rate of return to lower level City and Guild qualifications.

**7.17** The research also found that returns to vocational, though not academic, qualifications were higher for those with low prior ability. The returns to vocational qualifications at NVQ Levels 2, 3 and 4 for low ability individuals were double those of higher ability. This evidence supports the Task Force's view that there are clear benefits to providing alternative options for those less inclined to do well in academic learning.

**7.18** In summary, this new evidence on rates of return suggests that the biggest employer demand for skills is at Level 3 and above, and that the market rewards for those gaining this level of qualification through a vocational route compare well with academic qualifications. It also shows that those with lower prior ability who choose to take vocational qualifications at Level 3 or above do particularly well on this route. For those with qualifications below Level 3, the evidence suggests that GCSEs are the most highly valued by employers.

**7.19** Since these estimates do not provide any information on subjects of study, they are unable to shed much light on which specific skill areas should receive further investment in order to maximise private (let alone social) benefits. Hence, this chapter also considers other recent estimates of returns for more direct measures of particular types of skill, namely, basic and generic skills

**Basic skills**

**7.20** We have highlighted the growing demand for skills throughout the labour market. Although there are many employment opportunities at relatively low skill levels, there appear to be few job opportunities for those with no skills at all. Even the lowest skilled jobs in today's economy demand some form of skill and at least basic numeracy and literacy skills. These skills also form the platform on which to build higher skill levels.

[3] Alternative estimates of female returns to HNC/HND qualifications based on NCDS and IALS data do not yield statistically significant results.

**7.21** The IFS/CEP study has also shown that there is a significant positive return in the labour market from acquiring basic skills, and in particular basic numeracy skills (Dearden et al, 2000). For example, if two individuals are similar in terms of parental background and ability, the person who acquires Level 1 numeracy skills - those expected to be achieved by the average 11 year old - is estimated to earn around 10% more than the person who never reaches that level. Furthermore, there appears to be a significant return of about 6% to those who do not acquire basic numeracy skills until they are of adult age (although the results underlying this interpretation fall just short of statistical significance).

**7.22** The same research suggests the wage returns to basic literacy skills are slightly less than those for numeracy. However, the possession of literacy skills is strongly associated with the probability of finding employment (even after taking account of individual differences in family background and individual ability) (Dearden et al, 2000).

**Generic skills**

**7.23** The report has identified that cognitive, communication, teamworking skills and generic IT skills appear to be the generic skills most valued by employers. Green (1999) draws on a survey of employees' own assessments of changes in the skills they need to do their jobs. He finds that increases in the need to have and use problem solving skills (e.g. analysis of complex problems, planning activities of others) and professional communication skills (e.g. making presentations) are associated with a positive pay premium for both men and women.

**7.24** Green's research showed no positive link between pay and certain types of communication skill despite the fact that employers regularly report a need for client communication skills and 'horizontal' communication skills (involving interactions with co-workers). However, he suggests that such generic skills may be particularly hard for employers to observe in potential recruits and that this is the reason why these skills may not command an independent salary premium on the external labour market. Thus the salary evidence is not necessarily in conflict with other studies which have identified a rising demand for higher levels of communication and inter-personal skills as well as computing and cognitive skills.

**7.25** Estimates of wage returns to simple IT skills - for example, using a computer to input data and print out invoices - point to a 6.5% pay premium for women and 4% for men who possess this skill compared to those who do not. For slightly more demanding, though still fairly basic, IT skills such as the ability to use a word processor or spreadsheet, the estimated wage returns rise to 13% for both men and women (Green, 1999).

# Wage differentials between various skills

**7.26** Trends over time in wage differentials to particular occupations might also be expected to shed light on the types of skill that are most in demand in the labour market. However, as previously noted, any evidence on relative changes in earnings needs to be treated with caution. The New earning Survey (NES) only provides data at an aggregate level on changing wage differentials across a bundle of jobs. The analysis in this chapter will therefore be looking at averages and we know that there have been changing wage differentials within occupational groups that we are unable to identify. A further weakness of the NES dataset is that it excludes the self-employed.

**7.27** There is a significant proportion of employers who do not raise wages in response to skill problems. This may be due to factors which prevent some employers from responding to skill needs by adjusting wages. For example, many employers are unable to do this because of collective agreements, which make it difficult to target wage increases on those areas where skill problems are most serious.

**7.28** Other employers may be reluctant to offer such wage increases because of fears that they cannot absorb the costs and some may lower hiring standards rather than use higher wages to attract more higher quality applicants. However, with enhanced flexibility in the labour market in recent years and greater trade union recognition of skills issues, it is reasonable to assume that employers, particularly in the private sector, have more flexibility in varying wages (or at least raising wages) to attract labour to meet particular skill needs.

**7.29** Essentially the analysis which follows assumes that the labour market is competitive and that the extent to which wages reflect productivity is the same across occupations. However, it is important to bear in mind the points made at the beginning of this chapter that relative wages may rise in some occupations for other reasons apart from excess demand relative to supply.

## Manual Vs non-manual earnings

**7.30** In general the widening wage differential between manual and non-manual workers has arisen largely because of a decline in the wages of manual workers relative to the average. This may be due to the decline in trade union coverage and power having a disproportionately adverse impact on the wages of low and unskilled workers. For example, trade unions may have sustained the relative wages of low skilled workers in the past in spite of their declining relative productivity.

**7.31** Also, as argued in Chapter 3, skill based technological change appears to have contributed to increases in both the demand for and *relative* productivity of non-manual workers. In this context recent technological advances have tended to act as substitutes for relatively low skilled manual workers while complementing the skills of more educated non-manual workers. Growing international competition from developing countries in many low value-added markets may also have led to downward pressure on the wages of manual workers in the UK.

**7.32** These arguments are consistent with those of Harkness and Machin (1999) who found widening wage differentials between the more educated, who are more likely to be found in non-manual jobs, and the least educated, who are more likely to be found in manual jobs. This research has found that during the 1980s and 1990s relative wages have moved significantly against those with no qualifications.

**7.33** Figures 7.1 and 7.2 which show the relative earnings of manual and non-manual workers (male and female shown separately) also show a widening differential. This suggests that there may have been some adjustment problems in moving from jobs demanding manual skills to those needed for non-manual jobs. Average weekly earnings for male manual workers fell from 92% of average male earnings in 1975 to less than 77% in 1998. For women the fall was from 88% to 68% of average earnings. This is consistent with an excess supply of manual skills relative to demand.

**Figure 7.1: Index of average male manual and non-manual earnings relative to average male earnings**

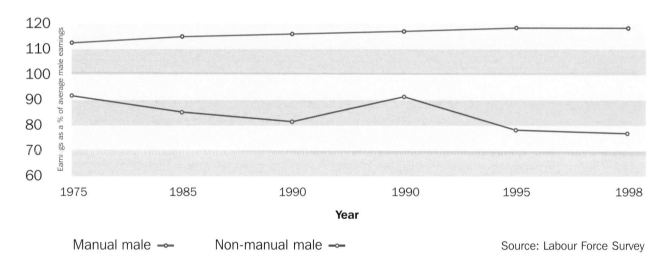

Manual male    Non-manual male                    Source: Labour Force Survey

**Figure 7.2: Index of average female manual and non-manual earnings relative to average female earnings**

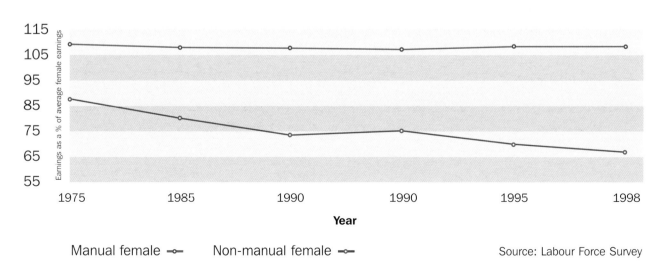

Manual female    Non-manual female                    Source: Labour Force Survey

**7.34** Weekly earnings for non-manual jobs did increase in this period relative to average earnings but not by much - for men from just under 112% to 118% of average earnings with women's earnings remaining static against the average. The relatively small gap between changes in average total earnings and in average non-manual earnings partly reflects the now very large and rising proportion of the total workforce represented by non-manual employees.

## Managers[4]

**7.35** Chapter 3 identified a rapid increase in the employment of managers and commented on what this meant in terms of the different skills needed. It made the point that the skills needed by managers were changing particularly fast at senior levels. On the one hand, general managers at high levels were widening their spans of command and needed to provide a more strategic role in delayered and more autonomous business units within their companies. At the same time there is a growing demand for senior managers of specialist functions (e.g. marketing, sales, IT) in companies where the focus is now the production, marketing and selling of core business products.

**7.36** Managerial jobs have always attracted a salary premium. However, from the early 1980s there has been a marked increase in the relative pay of managers. The salaries of male corporate managers increased from 157% of unskilled male earnings[5] in 1975 to 235% of unskilled male earnings in 1998 (Tables 6.1 and 6.2). This could indicate a shortage of skills needed in these types of jobs during a period when the demand for managers has been rising rapidly. Alternatively it could indicate a prolonged period of adjustment of managerial salaries which were relatively low during the 1960s and 1970s or a rise in their productivity as the nature of the job and role evolved.

## Professional occupations

**7.37** Chapter 3 noted that employment in professional jobs has increased substantially in recent years, with a particularly heavy concentration of such employment in two sectors: public administration and business and financial services. Chapter 4 noted the large growth in the proportion of young people entering the labour market as graduates though we have questioned whether the discipline mix of those graduates meets the needs of the labour market.

**7.38** Harkness and Machin (1999) found that changing wage differentials during the 1980s and 1990s suggest a shift in demand in favour of engineering and science graduates and against arts graduates. However, these categories of "engineering and science" and "arts" are very broadly based and the demand for graduates in the former will include new technology areas such as Information Technology. Chapter 4 referred to the Vignoles and Hansen (2000) finding that the relative return to engineering degrees during the 1990s rose 1.5% above inflation while the average return to all graduates did not rise above inflation.

---

[4] The occupational categories used in this chapter are based on SOC90 and are not directly comparable with those used in Chapter 3 which are based on SOC 2000. Earnings data by occupation are not yet available on a SOC 2000 basis.

[5] For the purpose of this analysis the term "unskilled earnings" refer to those employed in SOC category 9.2 (Other elementary Occupations)

**7.39** These studies are based on the degree subject undertaken irrespective of the career pursued. Higher relative wages for engineering and science graduates may reflect the premium the labour market is prepared to pay for the type of skills developed on these types of courses (e.g. high level numeracy) rather than rising demand within associated occupational areas. Indeed, earnings data do not suggest an excess demand for science and engineering professionals as a whole for whom relative pay has remained static during this period; however, this does not rule out the possibility of shortages in certain individual disciplines.

**Table 7.1: Index of male earnings by sub-major occupational group relative to SOC9.2**

|  | 1975 | 1980 | 1985 | 1990 | 1995 | 1998 |
|---|---|---|---|---|---|---|
| Corporate Managers and Administrators | 1.57 | 1.65 | 1.85 | 2.06 | 2.28 | 2.35 |
| Managers/Proprietors in Agriculture and Services | 1.02 | 1.14 | 1.25 | 1.30 | 1.50 | 1.48 |
| Science and Engineering Professionals | 1.53 | 1.57 | 1.67 | 1.77 | 1.92 | 1.93 |
| Health Professionals | 1.97 | 2.19 | 2.53 | 2.68 | 2.89 | 3.05 |
| Teaching Professionals | 1.58 | 1.43 | 1.58 | 1.69 | 1.92 | 1.83 |
| Other Professional Occupations | 1.46 | 1.57 | 1.70 | 1.89 | 1.95 | 2.05 |
| Science and Engineering Associate Professionals | 1.19 | 1.28 | 1.45 | 1.58 | 1.52 | 1.57 |
| Health Associate Professionals | 1.18 | 1.20 | 1.20 | 1.33 | 1.42 | 1.42 |
| Other Associate Professional Occupations | 1.45 | 1.58 | 1.71 | 1.97 | 2.07 | 2.14 |
| Clerical Occupations | 0.92 | 0.94 | 1.01 | 1.03 | 1.06 | 1.02 |
| Secretarial Occupations | 1.21 | 1.18 | 1.23 | 1.15 | 1.22 | 1.10 |
| Skilled Construction Trades | 1.04 | 1.01 | 1.00 | 1.04 | 1.08 | 1.08 |
| Skilled Engineering Trades | 1.16 | 1.19 | 1.28 | 1.31 | 1.39 | 1.42 |
| Other Skilled Trades | 1.08 | 1.08 | 1.10 | 1.11 | 1.12 | 1.13 |
| Protective Service Occupations | 1.20 | 1.35 | 1.53 | 1.40 | 1.42 | 1.44 |
| Personal Service Occupations | 0.93 | 0.96 | 0.95 | 0.90 | 0.93 | 0.89 |
| Buyers, Brokers and Sales Reps. | 1.18 | 1.27 | 1.41 | 1.47 | 1.49 | 1.51 |
| Other Sales Occupations | 0.89 | 0.89 | 0.90 | 0.89 | 0.84 | 0.83 |
| Industrial Plant and Machine Operators, Assemblers | 1.09 | 1.12 | 1.14 | 1.15 | 1.19 | 1.19 |
| Drivers and Mobile Machine Operators | 1.16 | 1.15 | 1.18 | 1.12 | 1.12 | 1.13 |
| Other Occupations in Agriculture, Forestry and Fishing | 0.83 | 0.88 | 0.84 | 0.87 | 0.93 | 0.90 |
| Other Elementary Occupations | 1.00 | 1.00 | 1.00 | 1.00 | 1.00 | 1.00 |

Source: New Earnings Survey

**7.40** For both men and women some of the fastest growing earnings in professional jobs have been in health and business and financial services. For males, health professional earnings increased from 197% of unskilled male earnings in 1975 to 305% in 1998 while other professional earnings (including business and financial professionals) increased from 146% to 205%. This contrasts with teachers' pay which is not really a product of the labour market. The more modest increase in teachers' pay relative to that of our unskilled reference group (from 158% of male unskilled earnings in 1975 to 183% in 1998) has more to do with public pay pressures than relative skill needs. More generally, the public sector is a large employer. If public sector wages are less flexible due to resource constraints, then this makes interpreting changes in relative wages more difficult.

**Table 7.2: Index of female earnings by sub-major occupational group relative to SOC9.2**

| | 1975 | 1980 | 1985 | 1990 | 1995 | 1998 |
|---|---|---|---|---|---|---|
| Corporate Managers and Administrators | 1.60 | 1.70 | 1.88 | 2.06 | 2.35 | 2.44 |
| Managers/Proprietors in Agriculture and Services | 1.09 | 1.20 | 1.31 | 1.42 | 1.53 | 1.53 |
| Science and Engineering Professionals | 1.92 | 1.88 | 1.88 | 2.07 | 2.32 | 2.29 |
| Health Professionals | 2.05 | 2.38 | 2.55 | 2.85 | 3.39 | 3.32 |
| Teaching Professionals | 1.96 | 1.73 | 1.93 | 2.10 | 2.35 | 2.29 |
| Other Professional Occupations | 1.86 | 1.89 | 1.95 | 2.32 | 2.30 | 2.39 |
| Science and Engineering Associate Professionals | 1.40 | 1.48 | 1.66 | 1.91 | 1.87 | 1.94 |
| Health Associate Professionals | 1.50 | 1.44 | 1.45 | 1.72 | 1.91 | 1.88 |
| Other Associate Professional Occupations | 1.51 | 1.58 | 1.73 | 1.87 | 2.03 | 2.00 |
| Clerical Occupations | 1.07 | 1.10 | 1.18 | 1.23 | 1.32 | 1.29 |
| Secretarial Occupations | 1.10 | 1.15 | 1.25 | 1.32 | 1.40 | 1.39 |
| Skilled Construction Trades | 1.31 | 1.01 | 1.01 | 0.99 | 1.48 | 1.32 |
| Skilled Engineering Trades | 1.28 | 1.2 | 1.30 | 1.36 | 1.58 | 1.65 |
| Other Skilled Trades | 0.98 | 1.01 | 1.01 | 1.00 | 1.08 | 1.05 |
| Protective Service Occupations | 1.57 | 1.66 | 1.92 | 1.92 | 2.05 | 1.97 |
| Personal Service Occupations | 1.04 | 1.02 | 1.03 | 1.03 | 1.09 | 1.03 |
| Buyers, Brokers and Sales Reps. | 1.25 | 1.44 | 1.64 | 1.57 | 1.78 | 1.85 |
| Other Sales Occupations | 0.82 | 0.86 | 0.92 | 0.93 | 0.99 | 1.00 |
| Industrial Plant and Machine Operators, Assemblers | 1.03 | 1.08 | 1.11 | 1.09 | 1.18 | 1.17 |
| Drivers and Mobile Machine Operators | 1.40 | 1.35 | 1.34 | 1.18 | 1.18 | 1.34 |
| Other Occupations in Agriculture, Forestry and Fishing | 0.82 | 0.89 | 0.95 | 0.93 | 1.01 | 0.96 |
| Other Elementary Occupations | 1.00 | 1.00 | 1.00 | 1.00 | 1.00 | 1.00 |

Source: New Earnings Survey

## Intermediate jobs

**7.41** Occupations related to business, finance, design and leisure have received some of the sharpest increases in intermediate level as well as professional occupations . Earnings of men in business and financial associate professional jobs such as financial analysts, tax advisors and brokers have risen from 246% of unskilled male earnings in 1990 to 302% in 1998[6]. Chapter 2 demonstrated that this is where much of the employment growth in intermediate level jobs has occurred.

**7.42** It may have been expected that earnings growth in IT occupations[7] would have been comparable with that in the business and finance occupations given the reported high demand for these types of skills. However, earnings across male IT associate professional jobs have risen more modestly from 182% of unskilled male earnings in 1990 to 207% in 1998. This may be partly attributable to the rapid growth of jobs in this sector with many new entrants starting careers at the bottom of pay ranges. Looking only at those with at least 12 months experience in IT jobs, pay increases have been above average, particularly in the last few years. Vignoles and Hansen (2000) do not find that computer science graduates earn significantly more than their peers - though, of course, many new entrants to IT jobs do not have computer science degrees. They find that computer science graduates earn about the same as those graduating in physical science, social science and business/administration though 24% more than graduates with arts degree subjects.

**7.43** Other explanatory factors for the relatively low increases in pay across IT jobs may include the fact that many reported IT shortages relate to very narrowly defined areas of IT skill and knowledge. In addition, some of the most highly paid and sought-after IT personnel now operate as independent contractors and their earnings are therefore not captured by the New Earnings Survey.

**7.44** The relative pay of craft workers has increased only modestly relative to the reference group of unskilled workers between 1975 and 1998. During the same period employment levels in craft jobs fell. Earnings in skilled construction trades have hardly risen relative to those of unkskilled workers (rising to just 108% of unskilled male earnings in 1998 compared to 104% in 1975). Earnings in the range of other non-engineering skilled trades have also be subdued (increasing from 108% of unskilled male earnings in 1998 to 113% in 1975).

**7.45** Relative pay for engineering related trades is significantly higher and has increased from 116% of unskilled male earnings in 1975 to 142% in 1998 despite the fact that engineering related trades suffered the biggest fall in employment of all skilled trade occupations in this period. Earnings data suggest that there are currently some severe shortages in some engineering related trades such as telephone engineers.

---

[6] Earnings data at this more detailed occupational level are only available back to 1990.

[7] A number of IT jobs classified as associate professional in SOC90 are classified as professional in SOC2000)

**Lower skilled jobs**

**7.46** The consistent picture for all forms of semi- and unskilled jobs is that relative pay since 1975 has fallen substantially. This could suggest a significant over-supply of low-skilled labour relative to demand. Even in sectors where employment levels have been rising such as personal service and sales occupations, relative pay is only on a par with that received in the reference category of the most unskilled jobs.

# Unemployment & skills

**7.47** The unemployed are one of the major sources of labour available to meet any unmet skill needs. Where genuine skill shortages exist, one would not expect to see a large pool of unemployed people with relevant skills. Where particular groups of people are becoming more likely to become unemployed one can conclude that the skills they possess are becoming less relevant to the labour market. The Labour Force Survey provides us with information on the occupation of the last job held (within the previous eight years) and the qualification level of someone who is unemployed. From this we can calculate an unemployment rate for each occupation and qualification type (i.e. the number of unemployed who have worked in that occupation/hold that qualification level as a ratio of the total stock of labour available for that occupation/ qualification level - employed + unemployed).

**7.48** This analysis provides useful information about those with skills least demanded by employers. One would expect their relative unemployment rate to increase over time. This type of analysis can also provide insights about the extent to which reported skill shortages in certain areas are genuine. One would not expect high levels of unemployment in areas of high reported skill shortage - unless of course those in unemployment with experience in skill shortage areas now have outdated skills.

**7.49** In analysing relative unemployment rates it is important that comparisons are made between similar points in the economic cycle. Employers tend to shed less skilled labour first in an economic downturn and recruit higher skilled labour first on an upswing. The analysis needs to look across the economic cycle to assess the relative demand for different types of labour - i.e. to control for these cyclical recruitment effects. The analysis presented below looks at 1979, 1990 and 1999 when overall ILO unemployment rates were at similar levels (5.7%, 6.9% and 6.1% respectively). One unfortunate drawback in looking at similar points in the economic cycle in this way is that discontinuities in occupational classification mean that we can only look at this measure of skill in a very aggregate form.

**7.50** Tables 7.3 and 7.4 both suggest that the relative demand for unskilled individuals and for those with no qualifications has fallen significantly from 1979 though 1990 to 1999. The unemployment rate of the unskilled rose by nearly 1.7 percentage points between 1979 and 1990 and by a further 1.8 percentage points between 1990 and 1999. The gap in the unemployment rate of the unskilled compared to the partly skilled has widened over the period from 3.6 percentage points to 4.5 percentage points.

**7.51** The relative demand for craft level manual and partly skilled individuals has worsened relative to those from professional and intermediate level jobs in this period. Similarly those with qualifications at Level 2 and below have significantly higher unemployment rates in 1999 compared to those with qualifications at Level 4 and above than was the case in 1979. The data suggests a clear trend towards a rising demand for highly skilled individuals with professional and intermediate level skills, a reduced demand for those with qualifications at Level 2 and below and for those with manual or low levels of skill and a much lower demand for those with no qualifications and with experience of only unskilled work.

**Table 7.3: ILO Unemployment rates by broad occupational grouping (1979, 1990, 1999)**

|  | 1979 | 1990 | 1999 |
|---|---|---|---|
| Professional | 1.0% | 1.1% | 1.9% |
| Intermediate | 1.6% | 2.5% | 2.4% |
| Skilled non-manual | 2.6% | 4.1% | 4.0% |
| Skilled manual | 3.5% | 5.3% | 5.6% |
| Partly Skilled | 5.3% | 7.3% | 7.9% |
| Unskilled | 8.9% | 10.6% | 12.4% |
| **TOTAL** | **5.7%** | **6.9%** | **6.1%** |

**Table 7.4: ILO Unemployment rates by broad qualification level (1979, 1990, 1999)**

|  | 1979 | 1990 | 1999 |
|---|---|---|---|
| Degree | 2.4% | 2.5% | 2.8% |
| Higher vocational/sub-degree | 2.5% | 2.7% | 3.0% |
| A-level or equivalent | 3.2% | 5.4% | 4.8% |
| GCSE/O level or equivalent | 4.1% | 5.8% | 6.5% |
| Other | 6.2% | 8.4% | 8.0% |
| No Qualifications | 7.1% | 11.2% | 12.4% |
| **TOTAL** | **5.7%** | **6.9%** | **6.1%** |

## Summary

**7.52** This chapter has demonstrated that, in terms of rates of return, degree and higher intermediate level qualifications are where further investment in skills are likely to pay the greatest dividend. It has also shown that both the academic and vocational routes to this level of qualification deliver a good rate of return. This evidence is supported by the analysis of trends in the wage differentials to different jobs. Those occupations which have experienced the largest wage gains over the last 20 years have been those at higher intermediate, professional and managerial level - occupations where those with Level 3 and degree level qualifications are concentrated.

**7.53** At a more detailed level of skills, it is hard to interpret what market signals tell us about relative demand for skills. Clearly, the finance sector has experienced one of the biggest increases in wages in recent years. However, it is unclear whether this is due to the difficulty that sector is having attracting adequately skilled people or whether people working in that sector are attracting such levels of pay due to the overall added value they are helping to produce. Certainly the extensive use by that sector of Information Technology, and the widespread evidence of skill problems for IT skills would, on the face of it, make large relative pay increases in finance no surprise. On the other hand the data on wage differentials do not suggest that IT specialists have received significantly above average pay rises - though the large influx of new entrants to these jobs may be a factor here.

**7.54** Relative wage differentials do not suggest an overall problem with skills in engineering though this is possibly not unexpected. It has long been the Task Force's view that skill problems in engineering are related to specific occupations and localities. This would not come through in the data examined.

**7.55** There has been a clear shift in wage differentials away from manual jobs towards non-manual jobs. Furthermore it has been shown that there are significant returns to skills normally associated with many non-manual jobs - certain types of communications skills, problem solving skills and generic IT skills.

**7.56** Those who have fared worst in the relative pay league and job market over the past 20 years have been those with the lowest levels of qualifications and skills. This is a clear sign that the job opportunities for those with this level of skill are limited. Where jobs are available they are very low paid. Evidence suggest that relatively small increases in the basic skills possessed by an individual (including that to which an 11 year old should be able to achieve) can pay dividends in the labour market.

## REFERENCES

Bennell, P. (1996), "General versus Vocational Secondary Education in Developing Countries: A Review of the Rates of return Evidence", *Journal of Development Studies,* vol. 33 No. 2 pp. 230-247.

Dearden, L. (1999), "Qualifications and earnings in Britain: How reliable are conventional estimates of the returns to education?" *IFS WP* No. W99/7.

Dearden, L., McIntosh, S., Myck, M., and Vignoles, A., (2000) *The Returns to Academic, Vocational and Basic Skills in Britain* (forthcoming).

Green, F. (1999), *The market value of generic skills,* National Skills Task Force Research Paper 8, September.

Harkness, S. and Machin, S. (1999), *Graduate Earnings in Britain,* 1974-95, DfEE Research Report RR95.

Psacharopoulos, G. (1994), "Returns to Investment in Education: A Global Update", *World Development,* vol. 22 no. 9 pp 1325-43.

Robinson, P. (1997), "The Myth of Parity of Esteem: Earnings and Qualifications", *Centre for Economic Performance Discussion Paper, No 354,* London School of Economics.

Vignoles, A. and Hansen K. (2000) *Relative Wages of computer Scientists and Engineers in the UK Graduate Labour Market.* Draft report to DfEE.

# CHAPTER 8
## SKILL PRIORITIES

### Introduction

**8.1**    The key aim of this report has been to identify the main areas where there is evidence of mismatches between skill supply and demand in order to advise on the priorities for future government spending on education and training. The analysis so far has mapped out the main trends in skill supply and demand and pointed to evidence on possible mismatches. This chapter outlines the main skill priority areas identified as a result of this analysis.

**8.2**    These key priority areas are:

- **basic skills** - those of literacy and numeracy, the basic building blocks on which to build other skills;

- **generic skills** - those transferable skills, essential for employability which are relevant at different levels for most ;

- **intermediate level skills** - specific occupational skills needed in intermediate jobs ranging from skilled trade to associate professional occupations;

- **specialist information and communications technology skills** - professional skills needed in the Information and Communications Technology (ICT) sector, and by ICT specialists in other industries - those 'e-skills' at the heart of the knowledge economy;

- **mathematics skills** - where we have a poor supply coupled with increasing demand for mathematics abilities significantly above basic numeracy;

- **major adult skill gaps** - the large proportion of the adult workforce with no qualifications or qualifications below NVQ Level 2.

**8.3**    The report has considered skill needs at all levels in the labour market including at the higher managerial and professional level. At the managerial level, the analysis was not able to identify specific managerial skills that were in short supply, but found a worryingly high proportion of managers and proprietors with either no qualifications or only qualifications below Level 2, and poor IT generic skills. These problems are covered as part of the priority given to adult skill gaps.

**8.4**    Part of the concern about mathematics attainment identified in the report relates to the way it limits the pool of more able students who are capable of undertaking higher level technology related courses e.g. in parts of engineering and electronics. The concerns that many employers have about the generic skills of graduate recruits, and an increasing call for some managerial skills for a wider cohort of the workforce, have also been referred to and these problems are dealt with under the heading of generic skills.

# Basic skills

8.5 The International Adult Literature Survey clearly showed the scale of problem faced on basic skills. To repeat some of the evidence quoted in that survey:

  - some 7 million adults in England (or one in five) are functionally illiterate - for example, if given the alphabetical index to the Yellow Pages, they cannot locate the page reference for plumbers

  - one in four adults has very low levels of numeracy - they cannot calculate the change they should get out of £2 when they buy one item priced at 68p and two items at 45p

8.6 Given the scale of the problem suggested by this evidence, it may have been expected that a lack of basic skills would have a more visible impact on the labour market than it does. ESS shows that, of those employers reporting skill-related hard-to-fill vacancies at the end of 1999, less than 15% of these said that the skills they were finding it difficult to find were numeracy and literacy skills.

8.7 This may reflect just a small part of the problem, a much bigger concern being those already in work with relatively low levels of basic skills. ESS also asked participating employers what 'new or additional skills' they would need to move into higher quality product areas and/or improve the quality of their existing products or services. As many as four in every ten employers included literacy and numeracy skills on the list of new or additional skills required to meet those objectives.

8.8 The labour market is already sending signals concerning the lack of demand for those without basic levels. Many jobs are closed to people who do not have entry level basic skills. Unemployed people form a disproportionate share of the population who lack basic skills. In a labour market where the majority of jobs require rising levels of skill, it is not surprising that those with low levels of basic skills or lacking the desired personal attributes find it most difficult to find jobs.

8.9 At the same time, there are positive rates of return to literacy and numeracy levels only marginally above a basic level. For two individuals with similar parental backgrounds and abilities, the person who acquires the level of numeracy expected of an 11 year old earns around 10% more than the person who never reaches that level. The wage returns to basic literacy skills are slightly less than those for numeracy. However, research shows that possession of literacy skills greatly increases the chances of finding employment in the first place.

8.10 Clearly, the supply side has responded to this problem to some extent. Qualification levels in the population have risen substantially in recent years. However, the UK still has a relatively long tail of people with low levels of basic skills. There has been a significant increase in basic skills courses, particularly for adults, to attempt to deal with this problem. However, provision is one thing, take-up another. Too many adults don't recognise they have a basic skills problem. Of the estimated seven million adults who are functionally illiterate or innumerate only 250,000 are taking part in a relevant course of study (IALS).

# Generic skills (including IT)

**8.11** People need to be able to adapt the skills they have and acquire new ones to be able to respond to changing labour market needs. Individuals need a platform of generic skills (e.g. to solve problems, to be able to learn) as a basis on which a range of more technical and job specific skills can be built. Most jobs call for a range of generic skills, personal attributes and technical and job-specific skills. The wider the range and the broader the base of skills that an individual has, the more adaptable he or she will be in the labour market.

**8.12** At the same time, the shift to a service-oriented and customer-facing economy is placing increased emphasis on the more socially oriented generic skills such as communication and team working skills. A wider range of jobs now involve some kind of interface with customers. More workers now need to be able to talk to customers to understand their needs (communication and problem solving skills) and persuade them to a course of action (negotiation skills). While the importance of all key skills is recognised, the analysis in this report identifies those of communication, problem solving and teamworking as being those most demanded by employers and where the gap between supply and demand is most critical.

**8.13** The growing demand for management-type skills highlighted in this report is part of the demand for higher levels of generic skills. In workplaces with less hierarchical structures and higher levels of employee involvement in decision-making, the ability to persuade colleagues is now much more important than the ability to organise and direct them. In manufacturing the reduction in layers of traditional middle management and the greater use of teamworking requires a much larger proportion of the workforce to develop 'managerial' type skills. These types of skills are no longer needed just by managers.

**8.14** The widespread use of IT has made the ability to understand and use IT equipment a generic skill. There are few jobs that make no use of IT equipment in some form or another. The level of IT skill needed differs from job to job. However, evidence suggests that a basic level of IT skill (e.g. the ability to input data and follow on-screen instructions) is a minimum requirement for 'employability'. Furthermore, a moderate level of IT skills (e.g. the ability to word process, use a spreadsheet and e-mail) is now needed to be effective in so many different jobs that these skills should now be regarded as generic as well. More complex or advanced level IT skills are in growing demand but usually relate to specific professional occupations.

**8.15** ESS suggests that many employers perceive internal skill gaps in terms of generic skill deficiencies, with particular reference to gaps in communication, customer handling and team-working skills in particular. Similarly when employers were asked to consider the skills they would most need to improve their products or services these same skills were highest on the list of those required. In many cases improved generic skills are sought in combination with technical and practical skills.

**8.16** This report has identified generic skills as a key skill priority area because evidence suggests that the response to the demand for these skills from the labour market is not adequate. There still seems to be confusion about how best to develop generic skills. The role of extra-curricular activities such as work experience in developing generic skills has not yet been adequately specified. The current level of generic IT skills among the adult population is unlikely to be adequate to meet future skill demands in the labour market.

# Intermediate level skills

**8.17** The evidence on intermediate level skill portrays a complex picture. Overall there is clearly a shift from lower level intermediate jobs (skilled trade/craft) to higher level intermediate jobs (associate professional). Employment in the middle (i.e. secretarial and clerical jobs) is fairly static but skill demands are changing, as observed. However, this shift from low level intermediate jobs to higher level jobs is now being driven by a change in the nature of jobs carried out at this level rather than the changing industrial mix of the economy.

**8.18** Nearly all the net growth in the demand for intermediate level skills in the past 25 years has come in "new jobs" such as design, finance and business services and leisure. Much of this has been in the service sector but not exclusively; there has also been a significant growth of these types of jobs in the manufacturing sector. These jobs demand a different mix of skills from those normally associated with intermediate level jobs. They demand creativity, communication skills and the ability to solve business problems.

**8.19** In production jobs (i.e. that part of manufacturing, construction and transport employment directly related to production/distribution) the deployment of labour between associate professional/technician and craft skills has not changed significantly. Both types of jobs have suffered reductions in numbers as new technologies and work practices have been introduced to improve productivity. The skills demanded of craft jobs in particular has changed as a result of the much higher levels of multi-tasking and multi-skilling associated with these new technologies and work practices. Falling employment has also been associated with reduced relative pay in many of these occupations.

**8.20** UK production industries are therefore very lean in terms of the numbers employed. However, this leanness makes it difficult to find the necessary skills to deal with significant increases in orders due to surges in economic growth. The ESS found that almost 40% of all skill-related hard-to-fill vacancies were for either craft level or associate professional jobs. The market is signaling a healthy demand for relevant skills in this area. Recent research has found that the rate of return to vocational qualifications most associated with craft and technician level jobs (NVQ Level 3 and above) is between 5 and 12% per annum for men.

**8.21** The UK continues to have a problem with the supply of qualified young people with craft-related vocational qualifications (Levels 2 and 3). As discussed in Chapter 4, the apparent progress made by the UK in the qualification levels of young people is misleading. Young people in France and, especially Germany, study for longer periods to gain qualifications - particularly vocational qualifications. Looking at the more comparable 25-28 age group we see that there is a considerable gap between the UK and France and, and more so between the UK and Germany in the proportion of this age group with Level 2 and Level 3 qualifications. This gap is particularly significant if we focus on vocational qualifications where Germany has double the proportion of 25-28 year olds at Level 2 and treble the proportion at Level 3 compared with the UK.

**8.22** Poor image/job security (related to past job losses) and low relative pay are at the root of many skill problems. In addition, in both manufacturing and services, the intermediate skills most valued by employers typically require lengthy programmes of employment-based training for their development. In the past intermediate skill supplies in Britain have been hard hit by periods of recession which have caused many employers to cut back on costly long-duration training - thus storing up problems for the future. This problem is compounded by fewer people taking traditional technician level qualifications (for example, the number gaining HNC/HND diplomas awarded by EdExcel in engineering has fallen by over 40% since 1989/90).

**8.23** Many jobs in higher intermediate occupations are now filled by graduates. This partly reflects the decline in the vocational route into these types of jobs in manufacturing referred to above. It also reflects the growth of "new" higher intermediate level jobs in the service sector where graduate level entry is much more common. The report has highlighted the potential drawbacks to the recruitment of graduates to these types of jobs. Employers complain about quality of graduates applying for technical jobs, referring to a lack of work experience, commercial understanding and generic skills. These are often the skills most readily acquired through employment-based training - learning experiences graduates have limited access to.

## Information and communication technology specialist skills

**8.24** Nearly all businesses are now dependent to some extent on Information and Communications Technologies. These technologies are being applied to an increasingly diverse range of services and manufactured goods. The Internet is revolutionising the way business is conducted. Technological developments are driving constant product and service innovation as firms seek to consolidate existing markets and develop new ones in the face of ever increasing global competition.

**8.25** Recent years have seen strong growth in the demand for ICT practitioner skills, particularly for IT skills, and especially for the most skilled group - the so called "technical architects". There has been a substantial response from the supply side, most notably the numbers taking computer science courses in higher education, which have more than trebled in the past 10 years. However, there are concerns about the quality of students entering Higher Education IT courses. The mean A-level grade of UK domiciled new entrants to Higher Education IT courses in 1997/8 at 14.4 points was 25% lower than the average for all courses. More students join IT courses through the Higher Education clearing system than any other subject.

**8.26** We expect there to be continued reports from employers of difficulties in obtaining specific kinds of IT skills and work experience. In part this will be an inevitable consequence of the fast changing nature of technology creating new demand for software and equipment skills faster than the supply side can respond. The problem will be compounded by limited numbers with the most sought-after ICT skills. Many employers continue to seek ready-made skills and relevant experience on the open market rather than develop it in-house.

**8.27** Another factor limiting the supply is the low numbers of women entering ICT jobs. Only one third of the ICT workforce is female - and this proportion is actually declining. Only 20% of students on IT-related University courses are women.

# Mathematics

**8.28** The ability to work with numbers and solve problems based on mathematical constructs is a vital underpinning skill for many occupations. Furthermore, employers seem to consider that the learning and practice of mathematics develop more general problem solving and systems thinking skills that are extremely valuable in the labour market.

**8.29** It is for this reason that people with qualifications in mathematics-based subjects such as physics and engineering are so attractive to other sectors such as finance. Research shows that young adults with A-level maths earn a significantly higher wage - up by some 10% compared to those with only GCSE maths or lower.

**8.30** The root of the problem is that the UK does not produce a sufficient pool of young people with good mathematics skills. We start from a shallow pool at a young age - just 45% of young people gain a grade C in mathematics at age 15. Our supply of people who choose to develop maths skills beyond this modest level is very much smaller. Unfortunately, large numbers of young people elect to drop maths at the age of 16 and the result is that only 10% of young people take GCE A-level maths. In addition, the numbers willing and able to take physics at A-levels have fallen during the 1990s, thus reducing the pool of potential entrants to electronics degree courses.

**8.31** It is not surprising, therefore that at the highest levels there are problems in filling courses which demand a good knowledge of maths and/or physics. There are only as many new entrants to Higher Education engineering courses now as there were in 1985 despite the rapid expansion in Higher Education provision in this period. Only just over 1% of those gaining a first degree in 1998 gained a degree in mathematics - only half the numbers graduating in history. This leaves us with a limited pool of the best people with the skills demanded in a wide range of essential jobs in the economy.

# Major adult skill gaps

**8.32** Despite the growth in qualifications discussed in Chapter 4, the majority of the workforce still have low levels of qualifications. For over half the workforce the highest qualification held is NVQ Level 2 and for one-third the highest qualification is NVQ Level 1. The report has demonstrated that France and Germany had one-third more of their workforce qualified to Level 2 compared to the UK and that Germany had double the proportion of the UK qualified to Level 3.

**8.33** Furthermore, given that much of the growth in qualifications is due to rising attainment amongst young people it is not surprising that the likelihood of holding a qualification falls with age. A 40-49 year old is just over twice as likely to possess no formal qualifications compared to a 20-29 year old; and a 50-59 year old is almost four times as likely to possess none.

**8.34** Inevitably a focus on formal qualifications is likely to understate the skill levels of older workers given the greater likelihood of formal learning (most commonly undertaken by the young) to be linked to qualifications and certified in recent years. Nevertheless even where workers have acquired sound job-specific skills over many years they can often lack the complementary broader knowledge and understanding and wider generic skills. Consequently they can be vulnerable to changing labour market circumstances affecting their existing jobs and unable to make the transition to new jobs.

8.35 A significant proportion of adults have no interest in further learning.  This lack of demand for learning is likely to act as a barrier to further development for people with low levels of skill as much as it is for those lacking basic skills.  Pressures from work and family were quoted by one in five of those reported in NALS as reasons for not participating in learning .  However, a lack of confidence related to age and ability and ignorance about opportunities were quoted by similar proportions.  This suggests that better guidance or counselling could persuade some of these adults about the merits of further learning.

# ANNEX A
## SKILLS TASK FORCE MEMBERS

| Name | Organisation | Position |
|------|-------------|----------|
| Chris Humphries CBE (Chairman) | British Chambers of Commerce | Director General |
| Llew Aviss | Llew Aviss Associates | Managing Director |
| Rita Britton | Pollyanna (Barnsley) Limited | Director |
| Eric Drewery | ABB Limited | Chief Executive |
| Tony Dubbins | Graphical, Paper & Media Union | General Secretary |
| John Edmonds | GMB | Chief Executive |
| Denise Hall | BT plc | General Manager |
| Sir Ken Jackson | AEEU | General Secretary |
| Dr DeAnne Julius | Bank Of England | Member Monetary Policy Committee |
| Eddie MacIntyre | Birmingham College of Food, Tourism and Creative Studies | Principal |
| Ashwin Mistry OBE | Brett & Randall Ltd | Director Board Member Leicestershire TEC |
| John V Palmer | Steel Training Ltd | Chairman |
| Peter Rainbird CBE | Rainbird Group | Chairman/Chief Executive Chairman, Essex TEC |
| Iain Roxburgh | Coventry City Council | Chief Executive & Town Clerk |
| Sharon Studer | 3 COM Europe Ltd | Vice President |
| Julia Tinsley | Pitman Training Centre | Director |
| Adair Turner | Confederation of British Industry | Director General |
| Prof Leslie Wagner | Leeds Metropolitan University | Vice Chancellor |
| Anne Weinstock CBE | Rathbone CI | Chief Executive on Secondment as Director of Millennium Volunteers |

# ANNEX B
## SKILLS TASK FORCE RESEARCH GROUP MEMBERS

| Name | Organisation |
| --- | --- |
| Prof. Mike Campbell | Director, Policy Research Institute, Leeds Metropolitan University |
| Lorraine Dearden | Institute for Fiscal Studies, London |
| Dr Alan Felstead | Resarch Director, Centre for Labour Market Studies, University of Leicester |
| Prof. Andy Green | Lifelong Learning Group, Institute of Education, University of London |
| Prof. Francis Green | Department of Economics, University of Kent |
| Prof. Jonathon Haskel | Economics Department, Queen Mary & Westfield College, University of London |
| Dr Ewart Keep | Deputy Director, SKOPE, University of Warwick |
| Geoff Mason | Research Fellow, National Institute of Economic and Social Research, London |
| Ken Mayhew | Director, SKOPE, Department of Economics, Oxford University |
| Hilary Steedman | Senior Research Fellow, Centre for Economic Performance, London School of Economics |
| Prof. Lorna Unwin | Centre for Research in Post-Compulsory Education and Training, University of Sheffield |
| Dr Rob Wilson | Institute for Employment Research, University of Warwick |